In this research, I used materials from the World Wide Web as well as books and journal articles. All who wish to know more about the subject this book presents may find what they seek on the World Wide Web. Research over the past decades has placed my thinking in the middle of this phenomenon and as a professional teacher I have developed my own perspective. I firmly believe that true originality lies in a new insight to past information, and ingenuity in the interpretation of old data.

A wise King once said, ",,,there is no new thing under the sun," Consequently, in an effort to digest the mass of available material, I may have quoted some authors inadvertently.

Shinto War Gods
Of Yasukuni Shrine

The Gates of Hades and
Japan's Emperor Cult

By Isao Ebihara, D. Phil

Post Gutenberg Books™

an imprint of
GlobalEd AdvancePress

Shinto War Gods of Yasukuni Shrine
The Gates of Hades and Japan's Emperor Cult
Copyright © 2011 by Isao Ebihara

Library of Congress Control Number: 2011923487

Ebihara, Isao., 1958 –
Shinto War Gods of Yasukuni Shrine
ISBN 978-1-935434-56-6

Subject Codes and Description:
1: LIT008030: Literature – Criticism: Asian-Japanese;
2:ART504000: Art-Animation; 3: HIS021000: History:Asian-Japan

Printed in the United States of America

Cover Design by Barton Green

Published by
Post-Gutenberg Books™
An Imprint of
GlobalEdAdvance Press
gea-books.com or GlobalEdAdvance.org

Dedicated to my best friend

Elizabeth Reba

TABLE OF CONTENTS

PREFACE

The Yasukuni Shrine or *Yasukuni Jinja*, with the literal meaning "peaceful nation shrine" is a controversial Shinto shrine located in Tokyo, Japan, dedicated to the spirits of soldiers and others who died fighting on behalf of the Japanese emperor. [1]Yasukuni Shrine has been a source of many controversies for decades after World War II. Included in the Book of Souls are 1,068 people convicted of war crimes by a post World War II court. A total of 14 *Convicted Class-A War Criminals* (crimes against peace) were enshrined at *Yasukuni War Memorabilia Museum*, including two who died before a verdict could be achieved. The shrine's history museum contains an account of Japan's actions in World War II, which many considered revisionist[2]. The displays and exhibits as well as numerous pamphlets from the Museum demonstrate their position that Japan entered the World War II in order to build peaceful world without racial discriminations[3].

[4]Shrine officials denied the legitimacy of the Tokyo War Trial and maintained that those 14 convicted criminals were "martyrs" who gave up their lives after the end of the Great East Asian War (Asian segment of World War II), taking upon themselves the responsibility for the war.

The primary focus of my work is the comparison of aspects of Shinto, particularly Pre-World War II State Shinto to pop culture, or to forms, shapes and physical metaphors for spiritual, social and political realities or the holy war like jihad, or something similar.

1   Wikipedia: Yasukuni Shrine. Online at http://artefactn.wikipedia.org/wiki/
     Yasukuni_Shrine
2   Welcome to Yasukuni's Home Page (Yushukan Museum).
     http://www.yasukuni.jp/~yusyukan/
3   Yushukan Zuroku 遊就館図録 [Illustrated book from Yushukan].
     (Tokyo: Yasukuni Shrine, 2008)
4   Welcome to Yasukuni's Home Page. Online at http:www.yasukuni.or.jp/english/

As I made a comparison of the cultural and historical components of Shinto religion to pop cultures including *anime* or Japanese animations and *manga* or Japanese comics, I drew upon the work of Alan J.P. Taylor's *populist* or *"anti-great man"* approach and Carl Jung's *archetype* theory. Taylor viewed history as being made for the most part by average and ordinary citizens rather than being dominated by towering figures of elites, genius or heroes[5]. On the other hand, an archetype is a generic, idealized model of a person, object, or concept from which similar instances are derived, copied, patterned, or emulated[6].

Archetypes emerged from the collective unconscious among general public rather than heroes and great men. Moreover, heroes or great men according to Jungian theory are mere archetypes emerged from the sea of collective unconscious rather than real historical figures. If there was a model of a great man like Heracles, he could be a very ordinary man, but people's memory made him heroic and distinct. The story settings of *anime* and *manga* are closely linked with the collective memory of Japanese people and heroes there are mere products of highly talented and imaginative authors. These authors continue to produce stories based on myths, folklores and legends coming out of underworld stream of water in the psychic world. Therefore, this comparison will provide an insight on the nature of the Shinto religion linked to Japanese nationalism.

For instance, Original and archaic Shinto religion was animism, which characterized by the veneration of natural objects as in *Princess Mononoke*, a popular animation movie produced by Hayao Miyazaki[7], in which the historical setting was Medieval Age. In the movie, *Shishigami* represented a deity in the form of a deer that had tremendous power beyond a human's comprehension. He was greatly feared and revered by

---

5 A.J.P. Taylor. *The origin of the second world war.* (New York, USA: Simon & Schuster, 1983/1996)

6 C.G. Jung. *The collected works of C.G. Jung Vol 9.* (London, UK: Beacon Press, 1959)

7 Hayao Miyazaki's Web: Princess Mononoke. Online at http://www.nausicaa.net/miyazaki/mh/

the people since he represented the incomprehensible forces of the nature. On the other hand, Japan's State Shinto, a hybrid between original Shinto and Western modernism created in the 19th century was like *Shishigami* after losing his head. Lady Eboshi tried to control the spiritual forces of nature by killing *Shishigami*. *Shishigami* without head turned into an extremely destructive god of death.

Headless *Shishigami*, which destroyed all objects around him indiscriminately, also resembled *God Warrior,* a large humanoid made from a dark tar-like liquid represented in another great animation movie by Miyazaki, *Nausicaä of the Valley of the Wind*[8]. It is a science fiction with future time setting, in which *God Warrior*, a lethal, giant, biological weapons used in a huge destructive final war, destroyed almost all human civilization in seven days.

The focus of my work is interdisciplinary, combining historical, literary critical and social-psychological perspectives with pop culture studies. I have discussed religio-political problems around Yasukuni Shinto Shrine and Japan's nationalism along with the contemporary pop culture icons of Japanese animations and comics. I have a passion to apply the content to young adults who belong to "post-modern otaku generation." Articles from current publications have also been used to support my stance.

I also intend this piece to be social-prophetic in nature and challenge readers to think about a socio-political issue and spiritual matter. My primary mission field as a social prophet is North America where I have resided over a couple of decades. But I also have a sense of a special call to share religio-cultural issues in Japan and the Far East to North American readers and the global Christian community because Yasukuni problem rises in my country of origin and so gives me significant knowledge and experience.

---

8   Hayao Miyazaki's Web: Nausicaä of the Valley of the Wind. Online at
     http://www.nausicaa.net/miyazaki/nausicaa/

For Christians who reside in Japan or other parts of the Far East, this information will encourage them to integrate the information to build coping strategies to deal with Yasukuni's agenda. For the Christian and non-Christian in North America and in the rest of the world, the information will increase awareness of what is going on in the different parts of the global village. Yasukuni's agenda will affect the life of global citizens no matter what kind of faith or religion.

The cause of Yasukuni Shrine and its War Memorabilia Museum is considered extremist and not likely to be supported by Japan's general public as a symbol of Japanese national identity. Yet, it has a consistent and solid support from the nation's right-wing establishment with economic and political power. The presence of Yasukuni Shrine as the centre of Japan's nationalism will continue to affect the nation's diplomatic relationship with both China and South Korea, and potentially cause economic and political turmoil in the neighboring regions as a result.

At the same time, the cause of Yasukuni is also supported by several groups of [9]*yakuza uyoku* or extreme ultra-nationalists with a linkage with *yakuza* or Japanese mafias and criminal syndicates. *Yakuza* groups have a silent coercive power toward Japan's general population since average citizens fear them greatly as the untouchables because of their extremely violent and cruel nature. In the past those from *yakuza uyoku* groups terrorized and assassinated several leaders who belonged to political groups with the range from left-wing to moderately conservative. Therefore, many of Japan's citizens are also reluctant to openly criticize Yasukuni's cause and fear the attacks from *yakuza uyoku* who support Yasukuni.

---

9   They are *uyoku* or right-wing extremist with yakuza or mafia connection. They are also called *ninkyo uyoku*.

CHAPTER 1

INTRODUCTION

Today, as in June of 1869, Yasukuni Shrine stands on the top of Kudan Hill near the Imperial Palace. In the midst of the shrine's broad barren courtyard, is a very tall bronze statue of vice-Minister of War [10]Omura Masujiro (大村益次郎) (1824 - 1869) on a pillar. Omura presided over the modernization of the Japanese military, and died after being attacked by some furious Japanese samurai opposed to Westernization. He was killed by a blow from a Samurai sword.

After the Second World War, Shinto as a state religion was disestablished and lost power to control the nation. Many Japanese governmental agents expressed aversions toward the State Shinto. [11]D.C. Holtom (1963) states that:

> Governmental agents, however, speaking in their
> official capacities, have frequently interpreted
> existing legal arrangements to mean that
> State Shinto is not a religion, since under the
> national law it does not receive the treatment
> accorded to ordinary religions (Holtom, 1963).

It was difficult to classify the State Shinto as religion in an ordinary sense because it lacked the aspect of "voluntary faith." It took on more the form of a cult with de facto power enforced on the entire nation.

The Shinto stood in a peculiar position in Japan. On the one hand, it had its origin in ancestor worship and animism in

---

10   Wikipedia: Omura Masujiro. Online at http://en.wikipedia.org/wiki/Omura_
     Masujiro
11   D.C. Holtom. Modern Japan and Shinto Nationalism, New York: USA Paragon
     Book Reprint Corp) p. 39

ancient times and therefore most Japanese view Shinto rituals not as religious rites but as mere customs or a routine of daily life. Shinto-based animistic belief and the praxis of worship of their ancestors and natural objects have been a part of typical Japanese life from the Yamato period. On the other hand, certain Shinto Shrines were not merely a part of typical Japanese animistic spiritual life, but closely connected with the ideology of nationalism and militarism based on the emperor system.

The primary focus of my work is the comparison of aspects of Shinto, particularly Pre-World War II State Shinto to pop culture, or to forms, shapes and physical metaphors for spiritual, social and political realities or the holy war like jihad, or something similar.

Social-prophetic in nature, the message is to contextualize the word of God into human society and challenge readers to think about a socio-political issue from a Christian perspective. For those who are inspired to be involved in missionary activities in Japan or other parts of the Far East, I encourage and challenge them to integrate the information presented here into coping strategies to deal with various religio-spiritual obstructs since knowledge is power when we are engaged in any kind of work or dealing with any task under all different circumstances. For the Christian and non-Christian general public in North America, I want them to utilize the information to increase the awareness of what was going on in the different parts of the global village, or think seriously what they could contribute to the globe as whole.

Saigo Takamori & Yasukuni

The Last Samurai (2003), a well-known Hollywood movie, has an evil character played by Masato Harada, who was somewhat modelled after Omura, a key figures of the Emperor Cult of Modern Japan. The character of Harada in the movie was actually a combination of few important key members the Meiji Government rather than real Omura Masujiro himself. However, the character did have quite a few resemblances to the historical Omura. All key leaders of the Meiji Restoration were eager to make Japan a mightier, stronger and more competitive nation on the same level as the West but at the expense of losing many traditional values.

Like the real Omura Masujiro and most other leaders of the Meiji Oligarchy, the character played by Harada hated the traditional values of the Samurai and tried to transform Japan's agrarian economy into a capitalistic and industrial nation-state modeled after the West. Most Japanese did not see Omura as a villain like Harada's character was positioned in the movie *the Last Samurai*. However, like typical leaders of Meiji Government, Omura was highly ideological, judging everything and everyone in terms of black and white, imposing the criteria whether the thing or person was a friend or enemy of the emperor and to the general Japanese public. So it is safe to state that Harada's Omura well described the darker side of real General Omura Masujiro.

On the other hand, [12]Saigo Takamori (西郷隆盛) (1827 — 1877), the real-life counterpart to Katsumoto, the movie's main character (played by Ken Watanabe), was also a pillar of a bourgeois revolution of the Meiji Restoration (1868) and subsequent modernization of Japan. He was excluded from the enshrinement in Yasukuni, however, because his actions were considered a rebellion against Emperor Meiji and his government towards the end of Saigo's life. Katsumoto did not tolerate the modernization that Omura and his colleagues brought about, so he split from his former comrades and started his own military forces in the province of Satsuma, his own native land. [13]Captain Nathan Algren, played by Tom Cruise, was originally hired by Omura to teach his soldiers Western Style military tactics to quench Katsumoto's rebellion. He trained an army of peasants and farmers in firearm techniques, and took them into battle against a group of samurai rebels led by Katsumoto.

In the battle, however, the samurai outfought Algren's poorly trained soldiers, and Algren himself was captured, taken

12   Wikipedia: Saigo Takamori. Online at http://en.wikipedia.org/wiki/Saigo_Takamori
13   Wikipedia: The Last Samurai. Online at http://en.wikipedia.org/wiki/The_Last_Samurai

as a prisoner to an isolated village. As he recovered from his wounds, Algren learned swordplay from a skilled sword master and conversed with the local residents. He also met Katsumoto and gradually became more sympathetic to Katsumoto's samurai cause. He started seeing Omura as a greedy capitalist and opportunist who simply wanted to transform Japan into a cheap copy of modern Western civilization.

At the end of the movie, as a large Meiji Government's army confronted the samurai's forces to put down the rebellion, Katsumoto and Algren fought side by side against Omura's army. Just before Katsumoto's died in battle, he asked Algren to bring his sword to the palace and hand it over to the emperor. Algren met Emperor Meiji, and described how Katsumoto died handing his sword to him. At the end of the story, Algren convinced the emperor that Katsumoto was always loyal to the Emperor and had a very honourable death. In actual history, Saigo did die, defeated in the battle, and his statue was erected shortly after his death, as many Japanese considered his act of rebellion as heroic. The statue can be seen today in Ueno in northeast Tokyo.

The Yasukuni Shrine, however, labelled him as a permanent and eternal enemy of the nation-state and Meiji Emperor Mutsuhito. It, of course, enshrined soldiers who fought against Saigo's forces and therefore died as gods. Yasukuni Shrine was a Shinto Shrine dedicated entirely to promote Japan's Emperor centered worldview, in which the Emperor was an inviolable divine-man and no Japanese subjects were allowed to raise questions about his rule. The standard of enshrinement was based on the degree to which the subject contributed to the Emperor Cult.

According to [14]Wikipedia, soldiers of Saigo's South West War or Satsuma Rebellion of the Satsuma province as well as those who fought the Meiji Restorationists from the Aizu

---

14   Wikipedia: Yasukuni Shrine. Online at http://en.wikipedia.org/wiki/Yasukuni_Shrine

prefecture under Tokugawa Shogunate in the Boshin War were all considered the enemies of the emperor and therefore excluded from enshrinement. This exclusion was deeply resented in both Satsuma and Aizu prefectures, and caused a deep rift among powerful and influential people in Japan for over a century. Those like Saigo who rebelled against the government were excluded from the shrine forever even though the general public in Japan considered Saigo and his followers heroic.

[15]Nihon Home Health Corp. Portrait, Saigo Takamori, 2010.[16]

---

15   Was available June 2010: http://www.kirei-ni.com/portrait/shouzouga/Gy-12sa/
      GY12-2.jpg
16   The picture is used under "fair dealing" (Canada) and "fair use" (USA) provisions
      in copyright law.

CHAPTER 2

ORIGIN OF SHINTO

Shinto (神道 – literally Kami's or divine way) was the name given to various religious practices with roots in prehistoric Japan. It was broadly animist, believing that a supernatural living force resided in natural objects such as mountains, trees and animals. The oldest Japanese literary works named [17]*Kojiki*[18] (AD 712) and [19]*Nihonshoki* (AD 720) were composed on a basis of the combined myths and legends based on the Shinto belief. Unlike Buddhism, Christianity, and Islam, Shinto had neither founder or prophet nor their own sacred scriptures, such as the sutras, the Bible, or Koran. Shinto was a polytheistic belief system that included a multiplicity of divine beings; therefore Shinto deities or Kami had some similarities with Greek and Roman gods. Both Shinto and Greco-Roman gods possessed human-like imperfections, vulnerabilities with capricious, temperamental and sometimes evil characters. [20]Sokyo Ono (1962/1969) a distinguished scholar in 1960 also contends that the ancient Japanese believed that the dead continued to live as spirits and from time to time visited this world, received services or rites from their descendants, and in return blessed them. This unique teaching of deification of dead such that humans could become gods for a great work or achievement, created the foundation of the Yasukuni Cult.

---

17   Wikipedia古事記. Online at http://ja.wikipedia.org/wiki/古事記
18   Wikipedia: Kojiki. Online at http://en.wikipedia.org/wiki/Kojiki
19   Open Encyclopedia. Nihonshoki. Online at http://open-encyclopedia.com/Nihongi
20   Sokyo Ono. Shinto --- The Kami Way (Rutland, Vermont, USA & Tokyo, Japan: Charles E. Tuttle company, 1962/1969) p. 109

Shrines

[21]Shinto was based on a unit called *jinja* (神社) "shrine" with its own history, *raison d'etre* or reason to exist, myth, philosophy and Kami or gods or objects of worship. [22]Shinto shrines were normally situated as part of nature, and different than a church or a mosque, with neither the characteristics of a chapel nor a place for worship; its sole purpose was for the enshrinement and worship of a Kami. In the last centuries, Kami has become enshrined throughout Japan. It was once believed that a *jinja* had been only a temporary shrine constructed for periodical festivals at a sacred place such as a mountain or cave, because it was believed that Kami would move around as much as any animal, and could not be confined to a single location. However, after a permanent shrine called a shaden (社殿) was built, it was considered that a Kami would take residence inside a shrine. Some believed that the practice of constructing *shaden* was from Buddhism; even today, many jinja from ancient times does not have shaden, but it was only a place to pray while observing a sacred place or an area that must not be entered.

A jinja today has several facilities within its boundaries, including a *honden* (本殿) and *haiden* (拝殿). The *honden* was the building that contained the *goshintai* (御神体); literally, "the sacred body of the Kami". The honden was reserved for the clerics or trained professionals to perform ceremonies and only the haiden was open to others. The honden was located behind the haiden and was much smaller and undecorated. Other notable jinja facilities were *torii* that serve as sacred gates for entering a jinja, *chōzuya* (手水舎) where one might cleanse one's hands and mouth, and *shamusho* (社務所) that was responsible for the maintenance of a jinja.

The Kami or deities of a shrine may be the natural object itself, one of the divine characters mentioned in the *Kojiki*, or any other legendary or historic person. In Shinto, each Kami possessed special characteristics, capacity and mission in the

---

21   Eerdman's Handbook to the World's Religions. (Grand Rapids, Michigan: William B. Eerdmans Publishing Company, 1982) p. 258
22   Wikipedia: Shinto shrine. Online at http://en.wikipedia.org/wiki/Jinja_(Shinto)

same way as deities in Greek, Roman and many other mythologies on this planet. For example, one could be concerned with the distribution of water, another with the manufacture of medicine, and another with harvest of crops or rice.

Sun-goddess Amaterasu & Other Significant Kami

[23]*Amaterasu* whose name literally meant to "illuminate Heaven" was the most significant deity from which the emperor of Japan descended according to Japanese mythology. She was born from the left eye of her father *Izanagi*, the creator god, as he was bathing in a stream, in the same way as Athena was born from Zeus's head in the Greek counterpart. She was assigned to rule the realm of the heavens while one of her brothers, *Tsuki-Yomi*, the moon god, was entrusted with the realm of night, and another brother, [24]*Susano*, a god of storm, was made a ruler of the ocean. *Tsukuyomi* was born from the right eye, and *Susano* from the nose of his father.

[25]According to Kenneth C. Davis (2005), Japanese myth described in *Kojiki* was a classic family-feud myth, and Amaterasu and Susano got into an epic fight. In one version of the story, Susano became angry because he had received what he considered a lesser realm, but in other version, Amaterasu and Susano fought to see which was greater. Amaterasu chewed Susano's sword and exhaled to create three deities. In response, Susano ate some of his sister's jewels and exhaled five deities. Traditionally, Susano was considered an extremely aggressive evil god with a short temper. In the past few decades, writers created numerous fictional violent characters based on this classical myth. In the video game Samurai Warriors, the character Sanada Yukimura's ultimate weapon is called "Susano," while the character Kunoichi's ultimate weapon is called "Kushinada," another deity of Japanese mythology.

Like Greeks and Romans, in Shinto there was no absolute deity that was the creator and ruler of all. Zeus in Greek (Jupiter

23   Wikipedia: Amaterasu. Online at http://en.wikipedia.org/wiki/Amaterasu
24   Wikipedia: Susanoo. Online at http://en.wikipedia.org/wiki/Susanoo
25   Kenneth C. Davis. Don't know Much About Mythology. (New York, USA: HarperCollins Publisher, 2005) p. 387

in Roman) mythologies were the head of deities Olympus, but neither qualified as the ruler of the universe.

As previously stated, both Shinto and Greek deities represented natural phenomena, such as wind and thunder; natural objects such as the sun, mountains, rivers, trees, rock and animals. Zeus in Greece represented the thunder, Amaterasu and Susano in Shinto Sun and wind. The largest difference between the two was that while in Greco-Roman mythology there was a clear demarcation between human and divine realms, or there was no way for humans to become gods, heroic and illustrious men and women were deified in Shinto counterpart. As well, Kami in Shinto were a little more vulnerable than the extremely robust, immortal and powerful deities like Zeus or Ares. [26]Thomas P. Kaslis (2004), a scholar specialized in Shinto mythology stated that:

> It is curious, too, that the celestial *kami* are
> more vulnerable than immortal deities of
> ancient Greece. The ancient chronicles relate
> that Izanami is burned in giving birth to the Fire
> God, then dies and goes to the netherworld of
> the land of *Yomi* to decompose (Kaslis, 2004).

Izanami was a sister and spouse of Izanagi the creator god and stepmother of Amaterasu. She and Izanagi bore many islands, deities, and forefathers of Japan. Then, Izanami died as she gave birth to the fire god and her vagina was consumed by fire.

Neither Greek gods were completely invincible or indestructible like the one and only God in the Bible. [27]Cronos the Titan, once a powerful ruler of gods was defeated by Zeus his son and sent to the underworld along with his followers. Cronos himself also ascended to the throne by cutting off the genitals of his father Uranus, the ruler of the Universe, and dethroned

---

26   Thomas P Kasulis. Shinto --- The Way Home (Honolulu, USA: University of
      Hawaii Press, 2004) p. 84
27   Greek Mythology Link. Online at http://www.maicar.com/GML/

him. [28]Uranus, one time ruler of the universe, produced many extraordinary children who were great achievers, but he was not happy with his offspring. He feared that these children might rise up and overthrow him. He removed all his children including Cronos out of the palace and locked them inside a cave. Gaia, the sexually and physically abused wife of Uranus, gave her son Cronos a sickle with which to attack her husband. Cronos made a surprise ambush on his father and seized his father's genitals with his left hand and slashed them with the sickle using his right hand. After that Aphrodite, goddess of sexuality, came into existence as the severed genitals of Uranus were thrown into the ocean, where sea foam mixed with his blood and semen. Having emasculated his father, Cronos freed all his vanished siblings and became the king of the gods. This showed Uranus was not absolutely indestructible although ruler of the universe, however, we have to agree with Kaslis that the level of vulnerability among Kami in Japanese mythology was higher than Greek counterparts. Kami was more easily slain than Cronos, Uranus or any other deities in Greece. Izanami died simply by giving birth to a baby made of fire. She was as destructible as half-divine Greek demigods like Hercules. Half-divine Greek heroes were as powerful as full gods in some context and demonstrated extraordinary might and prowess. However, they had more defects or weaknesses than fully divine characters and died more easily.

[29]The story of Izanagi and Izanami has also close parallels to the Greek Myth of Orpheus and Eurydice, the mortal couple. In facing death, Izanami was as powerless and helpless as a mortal woman like Eurydice. After that, an extremely bizarre story followed. Like Orpheus, Izanagi was advised by the ruler of Hades not to look at her before they cross the river or leave his land. When Izanagi looks prematurely at his wife like Orpheus against the advice of the king of underworld, Izanami transformed into a horrendous monster because she had eaten the food of the underworld and was already decomposing. Izanagi was horrified

---

28   Kenneth C. Davis. Don't know Much About Mythology. (New York, USA: HarperCollins Publisher, 2005) p. 196

29   Wikipedia: Izanagi. Online at http://en.wikipedia.org/wiki/Izanagi

and frozen to death as he looked at Izanami's transformation into a monstrous figure. She was shamed and enraged, and then pursued him in order to kill him. She failed to kill her husband, but promised to kill a thousand of his people every day sending horde of demons after him. His lovely wife was transformed into an evil goddess or vampire-like monster as he saw her prematurely. Izanagi retorted that 1,500 mortals (humans) would be born every day.

Ironically, his response to Izanami became the reality of militarist Imperial Japan after the Meiji restoration. Thousands of soldiers were killed in the battlefields every day as they continued to wage war after war and newborn babies had to replace them as disposable soldiers. The Meiji government encouraged the nation to produce as many male babies as possible, so that they were conscripted and sent to the war right after reaching the maturity.

Jimmu the Divine Warrior Emperor

Emperor [30]*Jimmu* or *Jinmu Tenno* was the mythical founder of Japan and the first emperor named in the traditional lists of emperors. He was also known as *Wakamikenu no Mikoto* (given name) or Sano no Mikoto, born in the Kojiki according to the legendary account, on January 1, 660 BC, and died, again according to legend, on March 11, 585 BC. The Imperial house of Japan traditionally based its claim to the throne on its descent from Jimmu. He was believed to be the great-great-great grandson of the sun goddess Amaterasu. He was the archetype of Japan's militaristic warrior emperor and the two *kanji* or characters of his name *Jimmu* (神武), mean "divine warrior."

[31]According to the legend, Jimmu and his older brother marched eastward from a region of Kyushu Island with the intention of consolidating their power. After his brother was killed in battle, Jimmu pressed on, guided by a heavenly crow. His army continued its march until they finally reached Yamato,

---

30   Wikepedia: Emperor Jimmu. Online at http://en.wikipedia.org/wiki/Emperor_Jimmu

31   Kenneth C. Davis. Don't know Much About Mythology. (New York, USA: HarperCollins Publisher, 2005) pp. 385-386

traditional home of the Japanese Emperor. Jimmu settled there and made himself the first "King of Yamato." This title was renamed to "Emperor of Japan" after the seventh century. After Japan imported the writing system and political philosophies from China, the court officials learned that the "emperor" had a higher rank than the "king" in China.

According to current consensus, Jimmu was a totally fictional character as there was no monarchy at that time. Japan's highly militaristic tradition after the Meiji era made the legend of Jimmu the foundational story of the Emperor Cult upon which the Meiji restorationist political ideology was built. The ruling class of Meiji Japan accommodated and twisted the Jimmu legend in order to fit their political campaign to build a strong military of the warrior emperor and Kokutai, or emperor-centred, spiritual community. After the promulgation of the Meiji Constitution (1889) to the end of the World War II (1945), the Emperor of Japan was the *daigensui* or Supreme Commander of Army and Navy with each uniform of both military divisions, indicating that he was the warrior emperor following the tradition of Jimmu.

Formation of Primitive Shinto in Pre-literal Japan

Regarding the ways that Shinto came into existence in the antiquity or pre-historic Japan, there are so many unknown factors. [32]There is no consensus as to where and when Shinto religion first developed. Some scholars claim it has always existed in Japan, back in the mists of the Jomon period or Japanese pre-history from about 10,000 BC to 300 BC. Others maintain it came about in the Yayoi period (c.300 BC–c.250 AD) as a cultural product of a huge amount of immigrants from China via the Korean Peninsula. They brought agricultural rites and shamanic ceremonies from the continent which took on Japanese forms in the new environment. The dawn of the incipient development of the Shinto religion largely remained in mystery because its belief system came into existence long before the introduction of literacy to Japan from China in about the eighth century, so that there were no credible documents through which we could study its early formation. Regarding the

32   Wikipedia: Shinto. Online at http://en.wikipedia.org/wiki/Shintoism

origin of Shinto, however, [33]Floyd Hiatt Ross (1965) suggested its Shamanic origin. He contended that:

> In very ancient times Shinto rituals were
> probably strongly influenced by the practices of
> shamanism when a man or women became "*kami*-
> possessed." while in that state of possession,
> oracles or revelations were propounded by the
> shaman or medium concerning the weather,
> prospect for the crops, or courses of action
> which the villagers should take (Ross, 1965)

[34]Thomas P. Kaslis contends that even without written documents there is some archaeological data and archives to tell about the religiosity of ancient Japan. In his book, Kaslis states:

> From this evidence most scholars speculate
> that the ancient Japanese were animists — that
> is, believers in spirits who operate in both the
> natural and human domains (Kaslis, 2004).

Among the archives that archaeologists discovered, amulets were vital factors which eloquently illustrated the earlier Shinto practices.[35]Kaslis maintained that they used amulets to ward off bad spirits and invite good ones. He suggested a possibility that the way of communicating with the spirits followed shamanistic forms related to those of Siberia and Korea. The majority of Kami in the primitive Shinto, according to Kaslis, were *ujigami* Kami of *uji* or a clan or the tutelary deity of a village or geographic area. They were guardians of clans or extended families in the antiquity of Japan. Primitive Japanese believed that most *ujigami* lived in natural places such as a forest or a lake. Each *uji* or clan had its own unique *ujigami* or guardian during the Stone Age. These *ujigami* were always worshipped in shrines. Throughout

---

33   Floyd Hiatt Ross. Shinto The Way of Japan. (Boston, USA: Beacon Press, 1965)
        p. 58
34   Thomas P Kasulis. Shinto --- The Way Home (Honolulu, USA: University of
        Hawaii Press, 2004) p. 74
35   Thomas P Kasulis. Shinto --- The Way Home (Honolulu, USA: University of
        Hawaii Press, 2004) p. 75

the country, there were many shrines of this origin to worship *ujigami* in it. In the early centuries BC, each *uji* and area had its own collection of *ujigami* with no formal relationship between them. According to [36]Encyclopaedia Britannica, the meaning of *ujigami* has undergone considerable evolution over the centuries, mainly because of the historical migrations of clan communities in Japan.

The pre-historic, pre-literate Japan was a collections of clans and tribes without a central government. Each clan or *uji* had its own separate and individual Kami, and there was no such thing as the Shinto religion as a collective belief system. Following the ascendancy of the Yamato Kingdom to the dominant position among tribes in the archipelago approximately the third to fifth centuries, however, the ancestral deities of the Emperor of Japan and the Imperial family were given prominence over others and created a narrative to justify it. The Yamato tribe ruled the entire Japanese Archipelago, and the King of Yamato then became the Emperor of Japan.

Also during the Yayoi period (300 B.C.E - 300 C.E), as Japan moved into an agrarian society from a hunter-gathering community, having learned various kinds of farming skills from China, most people settled in the plains where they formed communities that farmed wet rice and vegetables along with fishery. At this time the *ujigami* in the primitive Shinto was transformed into a guardian for farmers. Regarding some characteristics of *ujigami*, [37]Ono (1962/1969), maintained that:

> These are ancestral kami that are the protectors
> of a given group, and those that are patrons of
> a given territory of clans, that is, social groups
> based on kinship. It is quite proper to ask what
> almost ant kami protects, but a clear answer
> cannot always be given (Ono, 1962/1969).

---

36   Encyclopædia Britannica: Ujigami. Online at http://www.britannica.com/eb/
      article-9074124/ujigami
37   Sokyo Ono. Shinto --- The Kami Way (Rutland, Vermont, USA & Tokyo, Japan:
      Charles E. Tuttle company, 1962/1969) p. 9

The sun-goddess Amaterasu from which the emperor of Japan descended according to myth, was the original *ujigami* of the Yamato, the *uji* that became the Imperial family. The powerful Amaterasu, a, sun-goddess played an extremely important role in agrarian Japan during the Yayoi period because of the amount of radiation from the sun essential for farming. Also, over many centuries, the emperor was revered as the high priest who served Amaterasu because his service was considered most vital and essential for the economical wellbeing of farmers. [38]Ono asserts that with the increasing mobility of the people and the gradual break-up of the clans the term *ujigami* was also applied to the guardians of the residents of a given area, not just the area itself. Thus, while in the very beginning lineal and biological descent was a primary factor of *ujigami*, later the common community relationship has came to assume greater importance.

By the time of Emperor Temmu (631-686), Japan was not a mere collection of tribal societies any more, but was unified with a central government. Around the eighth-century, Amaterasu evolved into the most significant Shinto deity in the Imperial Household, and exclusively for the emperor's family. Nearly one and half millennia later in the nineteenth-century, this Shinto state, the Imperial Household of Shinto, became the origin of the most diabolic and destructible State of Shinto - the Emperor Cult.

[39]Thomas P. Kaslis states that besides *ujigami*, the notion of Kami had at least two other associations in the primitive preliterate Japan prior to when literacy was introduced from China. Kami represented the awe-inspiring aspects of nature and the spirits of the dead.

Princess Mononoke and Awe-inspiring Nature

Japan's fertile land in which climate and geography are suitable for agriculture and fishery was highly benevolent to farmers and fishers. They could usually expect abundant harvest

---

38   Sokyo Ono. Shinto --- The Kami Way (Rutland, Vermont, USA & Tokyo, Japan: Charles E. Tuttle company, 1962/1969) ibid
39   Thomas P Kasulis. Shinto --- The Way Home (Honolulu, USA: University of Hawaii Press, 2004) p.75

if they worked hard enough. The islands were subtropical in the south and temperate in the north with quite consistent patterns of seasonal rain and predictable growing seasons. The sea provided an abundant supply of fish and seaweed.

Nevertheless, there were some negative sides in Japan's geography and climate. Because the islands were still geologically young, the country was almost always susceptible to the devastating effects of frequent earthquakes, volcanic activity, typhoons and floods. So although the natural environment was generally sustaining, devastating disasters could hit the nation at almost any time. Primitive Japanese people developed religious veneration of the natural world mainly because nature could often be capricious and tyrannical despite its ability to supply generous harvests. Nature usually acted as a graceful nurturing mother and provided farmers and fishers whatever they wanted. If she was in a bad mood or offended by careless and foolish humans, however, she took away from people everything she once gave. In such a context, people in prehistoric Japan developed their belief system on the supernatural and spiritual forces beyond their control and comprehension. They also developed various kinds of rites, rituals, and talismans to exercise the magic and attempt to control the supernatural forces that the capricious Kami or supernatural forces when they needed appeasement.

The move from the lifestyle of hunter-gathering to the preferred skills of agriculture meant the population abandoned the mountains and began to settle in the small plains within valleys. This resulted in the former mountain lifestyle becoming part of their folklore, legend and myth. The majestic natural objects like waterfalls, towering trees, rocks and animals in the wilderness became items to worship in the realm of myth and focal points for connecting with the mysterious power of Kami. [40]Sokyo Ono noted that the Shinto religion was inseparable from the awe and reverence to the beauty and majesty of nature. He states that:

---

40   Sokyo Ono. Shinto --- The Kami Way (Rutland, Vermont, USA & Tokyo, Japan: Charles E. Tuttle company, 1962/1969) p. 97

Irrespective of the enshrined kami, the shrines themselves cannot be considered without some reference to their relation to the natural beauty that traditionally has surrounded them. Shrine worship is closely associated with a keen sense of the beautiful — a mystic sense of nature which plays an important part in leading the mind of man from the mundane to the higher and deeper world of the divine and in transforming his life into an experience of living with kami (Ono, 1962/1969).

[41]Ono details how in Shinto, natural objects like trees, mountains, rocks and caves were worshiped in shrines. He maintains that the majority of shrines were located within groves or forests where people used to live in antiquity prior to the era of agriculture. The close relationship between trees and shrines could be seen in the ancient use of the word *mori* meaning "forest" to designate a shrine, and the word *kannabi* meaning "shelter" of Kami for the surrounding woods. Lofty mountains, according to Ono, also played an important role in creating an atmosphere of dignity for shrines. [42]A mountain, which was considered as the dwelling place of Kami, was called *reizan* (霊山) meaning a "spiritual mountain," or *shintaizan* 神体山 meaning a "divine body mountain."

[43]Thomas P. Kaslis noted that the animation movie [44]*Princess Mononoke*, one of Hayao Miyazaki's masterpieces, eloquently illustrated the theme of Kami associated with the awe-inspiring aspects of Mother Nature. This story takes place during the Muromachi Period (1336 to 1573), which is considered the transition time from the medieval to the early modern period. However, the theme of the story was rather more archaic and dealt with people's relationship with the spirits of nature in

---

41   Sokyo Ono. Shinto --- The Kami Way (Rutland, Vermont, USA & Tokyo, Japan: Charles E. Tuttle company, 1962/1969) p. 98
42   Sokyo Ono. Shinto --- The Kami Way (Rutland, Vermont, USA & Tokyo, Japan: Charles E. Tuttle company, 1962/1969) p. 100
43   Thomas P Kasulis. Shinto --- The Way Home (Honolulu, USA: University of Hawaii Press, 2004) p. 76
44   Wikipedia: Princess Mononoke. Online at http://en.wikipedia.org/wiki/Princess_ Mononoke

the Yayoi period in which they abandoned the life in forest and moved to the valleys.

As Ono stated regarding the close relationship of the forest and Shinto, the spirituality of the forest was a very important theme of the movie and *Shishigami*, or the Forest Spirit, played very important role. The movie also had the appearance of [45]*kodama* (木霊 or 木魂,), a spirit of trees from Japanese folklore, which was believed to live in certain trees (similar to the *Hamadryad* of Greek myth). Folklore also included that cutting down a tree, which housed a kodama, brought misfortune.

Shishigami represented Kami in the form of a deer that had tremendous power beyond a human's comprehension. He was greatly feared and revered by the people since he represented the incomprehensible forces of the nature. Shishigami was the ancient spirit of the forest who had a number of powers; most notably, the ability to give and take life. Those that Shishigami deemed to live would live; the lives of those Shishigami believed had lived enough, would be taken away. This ability was so powerful that whenever Shishigami walked in his stag form, plants would instantly come to life then wither and die. Shishigami gave a kiss to those from whom he took life and gently nuzzled when giving life to something. During the day, Shishigami resembled a great stag with many antlers and the face of a baboon. During the night, however, Shishigami became *Didarabocchi* or the Nightwalker of Kami with humanoid appearance, a god resembling a human made out of stars with a long pointed face and tentacle-like spikes on the back. He was vulnerable when switching from daytime to nighttime and nighttime to daytime.

Lady Eboshi, learned that the all powerful and invincible Shishigami became vulnerable when he switched from daytime mode into the Nightwalker. Out of her ignorance she believed that one could control the destructive force of nature by killing Shisigami. Eboshi was a strong and caring woman who owned a place called Irontown, where the iron mined to make steel, and then made into high-quality weapons. She was a woman with good intention but naïve, who wanted to help the people of

---

45   Wikipedia: Kodama (spirit). Online at http://en.wikipedia.org/wiki/Kodama_(spirit)

Irontown. She managed to kill Shishigami by shooting him in the neck during his most vulnerable time as he began to transform into the *Didarabocchi* from the daytime stag mode. His head was completely severed.

As this happened, Shishigami's body expelled a black ooze, which drained the life from everything in its path as it tried to get its head back. After Eboshi shot off his head, Shishigami became a god of death, which resembled *God Warrior,* a large humanoid made from a dark tar-like liquid represented in another animation movie by Miyazaki, [46] *Nausicaä of the Valley of the Wind.* Eboshi tried to control the spiritual forces of nature by killing Shishigami, but failed, and created a disaster. In wrath, Shishigami utterly destroyed the Irontown that Eboshi had spent many years to construct.

Princess Mononoke described the animistic worldview of the Shinto belief system, the realm of the spiritual beings in Japanese folklore of the benevolent and yet tyrannical force of the Kami.

Afterlife in Shinto & Kami as Spirits of Dead

In Shinto, some of Kami was represented by spirits of the dead who had been humans in their lifetime. This part of the belief system is what makes Shinto Kami distinct from Greek and Roman deities. Although Greco-Roman deities possess some similarities to Shinto Kami, their belief system had a clear demarcation between human and divine realms, that is, there was no way for humans to become gods. This seems to be contradicted by [47]*Kojiki,* the oldest Japanese literary work about the myth of the Imperial family and origin of the nation that describes how heroes in the Shinto myth and some other brave people became Kami after the death[48]. Regarding this seemingly unique "human-divine cross-over" after death [49]Thomas P. Kaslis contends that:

---

46   Wikipedia: Nausicaä of the Valley of the Wind. Online at http://en.wikipedia.org/wiki/Nausicaä_of_the_Valley_of_the_Wind
47   Wikipedia: Kojiki. Online at http://en.wikipedia.org/wiki/Kojiki
48   Wikipedia古事記. Online at http://ja.wikipedia.org/wiki/古事記
49   Thomas P Kasulis. Shinto --- The Way Home (Honolulu, USA: University of Hawaii Press, 2004) p. 84

The relationship between the celestial *kami*
and humans is unlike that of certain traditions
familiar from Western mythology. The celestial
kami are not an order of being separate from
humans; the two are part of a shared lineage.
Thus a Japanese man like Michizane (Sugawara)
can become a kami whereas a Greek human
was often punished for aspiring to be godlike. For
Shinto, if the person has a pure mindful heart the
kami is discovered within oneself (Kaslis, 2004).

[50]Sugawara Michizane (845 - 903) was a scholar, poet, and politician of the Heian Period of Japan. He was also known as a patron for students like Saint Nicholas in the West. Because he endeavored to support students during his academic and political career, he was deified and enshrined as [51]*Tenjin-sama*, or Kami of scholarship in a shrine called Tenman-gu. In the West, Nicholas did not become a deity like Sugawara although he did transform into legendary Santa Claus. Santa enjoys semi-divine immortal status in recently made Hollywood movies like [52]*The Santa Clause 3: The Escape Clause* (2006), although he is not divine in the same sense as Sugawara.

In Yasukuni, those who fought for the emperor since the Meiji restoration, including Kamikaze pilots in the Second World War, were enshrined as Kami. These pilots, usually youngsters brainwashed by the ideology of State Shinto wanted to become gods, obtaining the ultimate honor and prestige from the shrine. They had the same kind of aspiration as [53]Mohamed Atta (1968 – 2001) of the Islamic al-Qaeda who crashed into the north tower of the World Trade Centre in September 11, 2001 and pursued the glory after death.

---

50   Wikipedia: Sugawara no Michizane. Online at http://en.wikipedia.org/wiki/
      Sugawara_no_Michizane
51   Wikipedia: Tenjin. Online at http://en.wikipedia.org/wiki/Tenjin_%28kami%29
52   The Santa Clause 3: The Escape Clause (2006). Online at http://www.imdb.com/
      title/tt0452681/
53   Wikipedia: Mohamed Atta. Online at http://en.wikipedia.org/wiki/Mohammed_Atta

It is interesting to note that [54]Kunio Yanagida[55] (1962) maintained that those who died unusual, unfortunate and sometimes violent deaths who cursed the world in the moment of death were often deified and became Kami. [56]Kamikaze (神風 - literally: "god-wind"; common translation: "divine wind")[57] pilots, convicted and executed War Criminals and Mohamed Atta, though he knew nothing about Shinto, belong to the same category of seeking transformation from death into a powerful and invincible spiritual entity. According to this logic, the negative psychic energy was generated in the moment of death for both Shinto and al-Queda.

Although some dead were believed to have been deified and provide the same living services and rites as Kami, the primitive Shinto generally considered death a curse and unclean event. Regarding the Shinto view on death, [58]Ono states that Shinto regarded life as good, death as evil and a curse, according to the word *kegare* (穢), which meant "abnormality" or "misfortune." The Shinto religion had developed numerous taboos and stigmas concerning the death.

There was not only one picture about the afterlife in Shinto worldview. According to *Kojiki*, the souls of the dead were expected to go to the dark afterlife, the *Land of Yomi*. This was like a Hades where all dead were going, regardless of the conducts during their lifetime. This idea of Yomi or Hades that both good and bad people were destined to go was obviously not comforting for most Japanese. So most of these ideas or rituals centreing on death were derived from Buddhism that was imported from China around the seventh-century. [59]Thomas P. Kaslis states:

---

54   Wikipedia: Kunio Yanagita. Online at http://en.wikipedia.org/wiki/Yanagita_Kunio
55   Kunio Yanagita. Hito o kami ni matsuru hushu [The custom of venerating a person as a kami]. Teihon Yanagita Kunio Shu (Tokyo: Chikuma Shoten, 1962)
56   Kamikaze (神風) meant "divine wind." The word kamikaze originated as the name of major typhoons in 1274 and 1281, which dispersed Mongolian invasion fleets.
57   Wikipedia: Kamikaze. Online at http://en.wikipedia.org/wiki/Kamikaze
58   Sokyo Ono. Shinto --- The Kami Way (Rutland, Vermont, USA & Tokyo, Japan: Charles E. Tuttle company, 1962/1969) p. 108
59   Thomas P Kasulis. Shinto --- The Way Home (Honolulu, USA: University of Hawaii Press, 2004) p. 76

> For relatives and friends in preliterate Japan,
> it cannot have been very consoling to think
> of the deceased as residing permanently in
> Shinto's Land of Yomi. Buddhist doctrine, by
> contrast, introduced the notion of heavens and
> hells as a system of reward and punishment,
> as well as the general idea of rebirth. Buddhist
> rites guided the deceased in negotiating the
> transmigrations beginning after death. As
> time passed, Japanese funerary rites became
> increasingly a Buddhist domain (Kaslis, 2004).

After the introduction of Buddhism and literacy around the seventh century, Japan became a society with the dual faith of Shinto and Buddhism. These coexisted in a very unique way. People usually conduct funerals in Buddhist temples because they didn't want to go to the *Land of Yomi*. But for most other occasions like weddings, New Year's celebrations and other ceremonies like the harvest rite, they retain their Shinto faith and continue these rituals as their ancestors did from antiquity.

Introduction of Literacy to Japan

[60]After the seventh-century, a writing system was finally introduced to Japan from China. This was originally used by Chinese who lived in Japan during the early Christian era. But it was the *Nara Period* (710-794) that saw the first signs of a tangible culture and it was during this time that the first historical records were kept. The city of Nara was the first metropolitan capital of Japan and it was considerably larger than the city is today. Under [61]*Shotoku Taishi* (聖德太子) Prince Shotoku (574-622) a regent, the son of [62]Emperor Yōmei who died in 587, and nephew of [63]Empress Suiko (554–628), the country established a constitution and a centralized Imperial state system.

---

60   Yaeko Sato Habein. The history of the Japanese written language (Tokyo, Japan: University of Tokyo Press, 1984)
61   Wikipedia: Prince Shōtoku. Online at http://en.wikipedia.org/wiki/Prince_Shotoku
62   Wikipedia: Emperor Yōmei. Online at http://en.wikipedia.org/wiki/Emperor_ Yomei_of_Japan
63   Wikipedia: Empress Suiko. Online at http://en.wikipedia.org/wiki/Empress_Suiko

The culture of the Imperial court was heavily influenced by Chinese political philosophies, which arrived via Korea and passed through the capital to the rest of the country. During the Nara Period, Japan acquired various skills from the continent such as weaving, metalworking, tanning and shipbuilding as well as medicine, astronomy and *kanji*, the Chinese ideographic form of writing. Confucianism was also introduced at this time. At this time the educated Japanese people began to study Chinese to acquire new knowledge and information not available in their country and write down what they studied, so that they could teach the next generation.

[64]The earliest known examples of Japanese writing, dating back to the 5th and 6th Centuries A.D., were proper names inscribed with Chinese characters on a mirror (鏡) and a sword (劍). But by the eighth and ninth centuries A.D., Chinese characters began to be used to represent the Japanese language. Since the two verbal languages are so different in their syntax and phonology, Chinese loanwords and characters began to be "Japanified" for more convenient use.

Characters that Japan imported from the continent were called *kanji* (漢字). *Kanji*, which referred to the Chinese characters used in Chinese, Japanese and Korean writing systems. They were considered to have originated along the Yellow River in China, around 2000 B.C. People in ancient East Asia used these characters with the rite of divination or magic as cracks on burned bones were interpreted as real objects, giving a written representation of that object. Kanji were pictographs evolved from pictures or drawings of real physical objects just as the *sun* (日), the *moon* (月), a *tree* (木), a *horse* (馬), an *eye* (目), a *woman* (女), *fire* (火) and represented meanings instead of sounds. Today, most characters require a lot of imagination to see the actual picture of what it represented. However, when knowing the origin of the character and its evolution, it is much easier to understand the picture.

---

64   Isao Komatsu. The Japanese people. Origins of the people and the language. (Tokyo, Japan: Kokusai Bunka Shinkokai -The Society for International Cultural Relations, 1962).

According to legend, the mystic Chinese emperor and supposed founder of the Chinese civilization, [65]*Huangdi* (黄帝) the Yellow Emperor, a cultural hero of ancient China, had a minister and official historian named [66]*Cang Jie* (蒼頡). [67] Cang Jie, as the legend goes, was tasked with creating a different system to record information. Observing all natural objects including the sun, moon, stars, clouds, lakes and oceans, as well as bird and beast, he created characters according to the special characteristics of the objects. After he had compiled a long list of characters for a written language, the God of Heaven was so impressed by this display of ingenuity that he caused grain to fall from the skies as a sign of his satisfaction with mankind. The legend portrays Cang Jie as possessing two pairs of eyes and four pupils, since he was an extraordinarily ingenious and insightful man capable of viewing present and future events.

After the introduction of the Chinese characters to the archipelago, Japanese eventually produced their own literature adapting the writing system to their own syntax and phonology. The earliest known literature written in Japanese was the [68]*Kojiki*[69] (古事記) (A.D. 712) and the *Manyoshu* (万葉集) (after 771). These works were valuable in revealing the evolution of the Japanese writing system from Chinese to a specialized system for recording spoken Japanese. The *Kojiki* largely maintains Chinese syntax, while using character combinations specific to Japanese for their semantic content. The *Manyoshu*, on the other hand, begins to use Chinese characters for their pronunciations to indicate Japanese words.

Around the ninth century, the Japanese created a writing system based on syllables: *Hiragana* and *katakana* (together: Kana). Of the two kana systems, hiragana is more cursive while katakana characters are quite angular. Both writers of *Kojiki* and

---

65   Wikepedia: Yellow Emperor. Online at http://en.wikipedia.org/wiki/Huangdi
66   Wikepedia: Cangjie. Online at http://en.wikipedia.org/wiki/Cangjie
67   Tatsuya Nagashima, ed. Nihon go kaiwa 30 shu II kyoshi shido yoko. [Teacher's Manual for Japanese in 30 weeks]. (Tokyo, Japan: PanaLinga Institute, 1982)
68   Wikepedia古事記. Online at http://ja.wikipedia.org/wiki/古事記
69   Wikepedia: Kojiki. Online at http://en.wikipedia.org/wiki/Kojiki

Manyoshu used a rudimental Kana system called [70]*manyogana*, which later developed into *Hiragana* and *katakana*. Japanese writings now consist of a liberal mixture of *kanji* and two sets of *Kana* systems that could be the most intimidating aspect of the language for new learners.

Hiragana and *katakana* are Japanese scripts and represent the sounds of syllables instead of the meanings. The 46 characters are the first step in learning Japanese writing. *Hiragana* and *katakana* each consist of 46 signs and have been strongly simplified over the centuries. When looking at a Japanese text, one can clearly distinguish between two kinds of signs: the complicated *kanji* and the simpler *kana* signs.

Among the syllables were five vowels あいうえお (a i u e o). The rest were syllables combined by one of these vowels with a consonant かきくけこらりる… (ka ki ku ke ko ra ri ru …). One exception was the ん (n), which consisted of the consonant only. In addition, they produce voiced sounds like "g," "z," "d," "b" and "p" by adding two small strokes or a small circle in the top right corner next to some of the characters.

Hiragana were made from Chinese character's *caoshuti* or a simplified form in the Heian era (794-1192). Since *hiragana* characters were developed and at first used mostly by women so they were called *onna de*, which means "women's character." At the time, the Chinese writing system of *kanji* was considered too difficult for women, as it required years of study. In this era, a female writer, [71]*Murasaki Shikibu* (紫式部) (c.973–c.1014 or 1025), wrote [72]*Genji Monogarari* (源氏物語) or "story of Mr. Genji," in *hiragana*, one of the oldest long novels in the world.

While *hiragana* was called *onna de*, *katakana* was called *otoko de*, which meant "men's character." Even Japanese students of Buddhism (mostly priests or monks and predominantly males) were having trouble keeping up with the

70   Wikipedia: Man'yōgana. Online at http://en.wikipedia.org/wiki/Manyogana
71   Wikepedia: Murasaki Shikibu. Online at http://en.wikipedia.org/wiki/Murasaki_Shikibu
72   Wikepedia: The Tale of Genji. Online at http://en.wikipedia.org/wiki/The_Tale_of_Genji

use of Chinese characters. It seemed that students taking notes during lectures often had a hard time with the pronunciations and meanings of the unfamiliar *kanji*. In order for them to be able to keep up with the pace of the lectures, a phonetic shorthand had to be developed. Instead of adopting hiragana, another purely phonetic form of writing had to be developed. An interesting change in the method of deriving the characters was the use of only part of the Chinese character for simplification since they required writing quickly for note taking. They were called *katakana* (片仮名) or side-characters, since they took only one side of *kanji*. This new form of writing was also much more angular than *hiragana* because they were originally portions of *kanji* that were not cursive like *hiragana*. *Kibi no Makibi* (吉備真備 - AD 693-755)[73], who spent over 20 years in China as a student, invented *katakana* by the simplification of a single element or radical from each of the phonetic kanji. Each *katakana* symbol was derived from a Chinese character in the same way as each *Hiragana* symbol, except that the Hiragana were simplified from entire characters. *Katakana* were initially used only as a pronunciation aids in Buddhist scriptures, but have been mixed with Chinese characters from the ninth century to the present. At any rate, *katakana* began to be used in fields of science and learning.[74]

[75]In modern times, hiragana and katakana have differentiated into distinct usages within written Japanese. Katakana is now used to write loan words, foreign words brought into Japanese, particularly those from the West after the nineteenth-century. Such borrowing usually occurred when the Japanese language lacked a native word to express a foreign idea.

Kojiki & Nihonshoki as Shinto Scriptures

Before the end of the seventh-century Japan made a dramatic transition into an established nation-state with a

---

73 *Kibi no Makibi* went to China as a young man to study philosophy, history, politics, mathematics, astronomy, music, and military and stayed there for 19 years, until he finally went back to Japan.
74 Wikipedia: Kibi Makibi. Online at http://en.wikipedia.org/wiki/Kibi_Makibi
75 Eri Banno, Ono, Yutaka, et al. Genki: An Integrated Course in elementary Japanese I, Vol. 1, (Tokyo, Japan: Japan Times Press, 1999/2002)

centralized government from a mere collection of barbaric tribes. The leaders during the era were extremely eager to acquire the literacy and knowledge from China, since it was one of only a few nations with literacy and advanced civilization and possessed highly developed technology and a state-governing system based on Taoism, Confucianism and Buddhism.

As Ono noted, in antiquity Shinto did not possess sacred scriptures, such as the Bible for Christianity or Koran for Islam. In the early eighth-century when illiteracy was on the decline, Japanese court officials produced twin-narratives named *Kojiki* (古事記) and *Nihonshoki* (日本書紀) in which the Shinto based foundational stories of the nation were stated.

The emperor's court drove almost all literate intelligentsia in the archipelago who had attained Chinese education, to complete these narratives. Japan's emperors/empresses and government officials including Prince Shotoku, Emperor Yōmei and Empress Jito invested a tremendous amount of energy to salvage their country out of the savage learning state with effective governing methodologies, literacy and technology from the continent. They also sent many ambitious young men to China and encouraged them to acquire new knowledge from teachers in a more advanced and civilized nation than their own to study.

Kojiki was considered the oldest Japanese literature to describe the myth about the Imperial family as it descended from the divine lineage and origin of the nation. Kojiki was written in a similar writing style as *Manyoshu* or the combination of *kanji* and the primitive *kana* system called *manyogana*, although the former largely maintains Chinese syntax. The *Kojiki* was presented by *Ōno Yasumaro* to Emperor Temmu (631-686) in CE 680, based upon the events that had been memorized from the previous book, the *Kujiki*, and by those who held the stories passed down over generations, and those memorized by Hieda no Are, the official court story teller hired in CE 712.

[76]Thomas P. Kaslis maintains that although both texts produced by imperial directives to record the origin of Japan and the emperor, they have different objectives and functions. He states:

> Both Kojiki and Nihonshoki survey the time
> period from before the creation of Japan to
> their compilation in the early century. Yet their
> emphases differ. Kojiki is rich in detail about
> the mythic preliterate period from the origins of
> Japan to the imperial rules of the sixth century.
> In comparison, Nihonshoki has much more detail
> about the emperors from the sixth century up
> to the date of writing. In this respect, the two
> narratives complement each other (Kaslis, 2004).

[77]Kaslis notes that these two chronicles contained the different roles that the Japanese court officials intended. According to Kaslis, *Nihonshoki* was written in Chinese because it was designed to present foreign readers with an authoritative document about Japanese culture and its religio-political foundations. The city of Nara was the first permanent metropolitan Capital that the Japanese had, and was modeled on *Chang'an*, the capital of *Tong* in China. Thus, the emperor and the court leadership intended to send the message to China and surrounding nations that Japan had changed and they were no longer a savage, tribal and illiterate society.

Kojiki, however, was not compiled to impress foreigners. It was Hieda no Are's task to collect the various extant oral narratives and weave them together into a single coherent story. [78]According to Kaslis, Kojiki was directed to Japanese readers and was, at least in part, a cultural preservation project. The writers must have intended to use Kojiki to educate and edify

---

76   Thomas P Kasulis. Shinto --- The Way Home (Honolulu, USA: University of Hawaii Press, 2004) p. 80
77   Thomas P Kasulis. Shinto --- The Way Home (Honolulu, USA: University of Hawaii Press, 2004) p. 82
78   Thomas P Kasulis. Shinto --- The Way Home (Honolulu, USA: University of Hawaii Press, 2004) p. 82

the Japanese public that was still predominantly illiterate and undereducated. Thus, by reading Kojiki, one could observe a passion and enthusiasm for the emperor and court officials to transform Japan into a literate, civilized and intelligent nation-state.

After the Meiji Restoration in1868, the leadership of the government used *Kojiki* as the sacred book for the newly created State Shinto to establish the divinity and inviolability of the emperor. The Meiji oligarchy carefully studied Western models of a unitary sacro-society in which state and the religion were one and inseparable, and came to the conclusion that they had to possess their own sacred scripture or Shinto equivalency of the Bible or Koran. However, it was far from the intention of the writers in the eighth-century.

Early Influence of Buddhism & Taoism

From the very beginnings in early formation, Shinto has been profoundly influenced by Buddhism, Taoism, and Confucianism from China and has made significant transformation throughout history. [79]Floyd Hiatt Ross contends that after the influx of Chinese influence, many Shinto ceremonies were modified, especially by some of the practices of Taoism at its popular folk level. At times, unbeknownst to most people, foreign deities from different religions immigrated into the Shinto domain.

For example, six members of *Shichifukujin* or "Seven deities of good fortune," reputed to bring good luck, have Chinese or Indian origins. Among them only *Ebisu* the god of fishermen and good fortune is Japanese Kami coming from Shinto mythology written in *Kojiki*. [80]According to the tradition in the Kojiki, Ebisu, formerly *Hiruko-no-Mikoto*, a sibling of the sun-goddess Amaterasu, was the third son of the Shinto gods *Izanagi-no-Mikoro* and *Izanami-no-Mikoto*, the progenitors of the islands of Japan. Yet since he was born without any bones he was cast out into the ocean at age three. Somehow he returned

---

79   Floyd Hiatt Ross. Shinto The Way of Japan. (Boston, USA: Beacon Press, 1965) p. 58
80   A to Z Photo Dictionary Japanese Buddhist Statuary. Online at http://www. onmarkproductions.com/htm

to land and was cared for by one Ebisu Saburo. He overcame many hardships and later became the god Ebisu.

[81]Other members of *Shichifukujin* include *Daikoku, Benzaiten, Hotei, Bishamonten, Fukurokuju,* and *Juroujin*. *Daikoku* with Indian Buddhism origin had been widely known as the Japanese god of wealth and farmers, although in earlier centuries he was considered a fierce protector deity. In Japan, artwork of this deity usually shows him wearing a hood and standing on bales of rice, carrying a large sack of treasure slung over his shoulder and holding a small magic mallet. *Benzaiten,* the sea goddess with Indian Buddhism origin, is the sole female among the Seven Lucky Gods of Japan. She represents the patroness of music, fine arts (dancing, acting, visual), and good fortune in general, and was often shown carrying a *biwa* or Japanese mandolin and playing a lute. *Hotei* had Chinese Taoism/Buddhism roots and was the god of contentment and happiness with a cheerful face and a big belly. He held a large cloth bag over his back, one that never empties, for he uses it to feed the poor and needy. *Bishamonten* of Indian origin was the god of war and warriors, and a dispenser of wealth and good fortune. *Bishamonten* was also considered a god of healing, with the power to save emperors from life-threatening illness and to expel the demons of plague. He was usually clad in armor, with a spear in one hand and a pagoda in the other. He was also known as a god who punished evildoers. [82]

The remaining two are deities with strictly Taoism traditional background. *Fukurokuju* was a Chinese god of wisdom, wealth, and longevity. He had an unusually high forehead, and is typically shown holding a cane with a sutra scroll (hebi) attached to it. *Fukurokuju* probably originated from an old Chinese tale about a mythical Taoist Chinese hermit sage during the *Sung* Period renowned for performing miracles. In China, this hermit was considered to embody the celestial powers of the south polar star or Southern Cross. *Juroujin* was a god of longevity. He

---

81   Wikipedia: Seven Lucky Gods. Online at http://en.wikipedia.org/wiki/Seven_Lucky_Gods

82   Seiyaku.com: Seven Lucky Gods. Online at http://www.seiyaku.com/reference/seven/shichifukujin.html

was depicted as an old man with a long white beard, carrying a holy staff with a scroll tied to it, on which is written the life span of all living things.

Regarding the Taoist influence on Shinto, [83]Tim Barret (2000) suggests the possibility that early Shinto prior to the *Kojiki* and *Nihonshoki* was influenced and synchronized by Chinese Taoism. Some Shinto Kami has very similar names and characters to those in Taoist myth. Barret maintains that the names of Taoist divinities were listed in *Nihonkoku genzaisho mokuroku* of Fujiwara Sukeyo (who died 898), one of ancient literary sources from Japan. Besides that, *Fukurokuju* and *Juroujin* of the "Seven deities of good fortune" came strictly from Taoist tradition but *Hotei* had both Taoist and Buddhist background.

[84]Barret also noted that the word *tenno* (天皇) that means "heavenly emperor" of divine origin was the Japanese term for the emperor, and therefore justified the myth that the emperor had a divine lineage that could have been stemmed from Taoist myth. In his article, Barret states:

> The history of the term *tenno* does illustrate
> some of the problems involved in talking of Taoist
> influence. Its Chinese form, *tianhuang*, was
> undoubtedly chosen as part of an ideological
> attempt to bend Taoism to the service of the
> dynasty, yet for political reasons (Barret, 2000).

[85]According to him, there is firm evidence that at the beginning of the seventh-century, Japanese relayed to China the information that their monarch was called by them *ame no kami*, "Lord of Heaven," a title for which the Chinese *tianwang* would be an appropriate equivalent. He maintains that the influence of State Taoism in China on Japanese ideas of sovereignty based

---

83   Tim Barret. Shinto and Taoism in early Japan. Shinto in History: ways of kami: University of Hawaii Press, 2000 p. 19
84   Tim Barret. Shinto and Taoism in early Japan. Shinto in History: ways of kami: University of Hawaii Press, 2000 p. 27
85   Tim Barret. Shinto and Taoism in early Japan. Shinto in History: ways of kami: University of Hawaii Press, 2000 p. 24

on divine descent must be carefully investigated and evaluated, because we have only a few documents to connect Taoism and Shintoism. [86]Barret also states there is another period in which the Japanese Government officially rejected the introduction of Taoism to Japan. However, we have enough evidence to prove the terminology and concept of *tenno,* or heavenly emperor in Japan had Chinese origins. The philosophy of Taoism seemed to have influenced and impacted Japan during its first few centuries, regardless of the attitude of Japanese government officials.

Shinto as a National Religion

From the Yamato period (AD 250–710), the imperial household took a central position within Shinto. [87]The newly established Imperial Household of Shinto had religious rites conducted at the three shrines within the palace grounds that were built exclusively for the use of the Imperial Family. Besides these three shrines within the palace, the Grand Shrine of Ise was extremely important for Imperial Household Shinto, because the principal deity there was Amaterasu. Throughout centuries, the Grand Shrine of Ise was generally regarded as the apex of all shrines. Worship there was considered the highest expression of respect to the Emperor and his family, and to all that was best in the culture, history and racial consciousness of the Japanese people.

In the book of *Kojiki*, royal ancestry was tracked back through legendary heroic Emperor *Ninigi*, believed to have been the grandson of sun-goddess *Amaterasu*. Amaterasu who was originally a mere *ujigami* for the clan of Yamato, became the most significant deity in the Imperial Household Shinto around the eighth-century. The powerful Amaterasu, the sun-goddess who had an extremely significant function in agrarian Japan during Yayoi period, continued to play an important role after the emperor became the centre of Shinto rites.

---

86   Tim Barret. Shinto and Taoism in early Japan. Shinto in History: ways of kami: University of Hawaii Press, 2000 p. 16

87   Sokyo Ono. Shinto --- The Kami Way (Rutland, Vermont, USA & Tokyo, Japan: Charles E. Tuttle company, 1962/1969) p. 13

There was a long period that the emperor's power became almost invisible after the ninth-century up to the Meiji Restoration which took place in the nineteen-century. During the long period of dormancy, real political power was taken by the [88]Fujiwara Clan, then in the late twelfth century, by the hands of Samurai class rulers.

When the monarchy was restored in 1868 to a central position in Japanese politics under Emperor Meiji, up until the end of the Pacific War in 1945, the Shinto religion was officially the national religion, and promoted the Emperor Cult based on the belief that he was divine and descended from Amaterasu the sun-goddess. During the period between 1968 and 1945, the ruling class transformed Shinto into a malignant and destructive force named State Shinto, which led the nation into insanity with a totalitarian regime and a series of wars.

The State Shinto was dismantled by the authority of the Allied Force who controlled the nation during an era of occupation after the Second World War. The emperor's semi-divine status was denied and he was officially separated from the Shinto religion and declared fully human under the government of Prime Minister Shigeru Yoshida. Nevertheless, Shinto remained as the "private belief" of the imperial household, although it was not an affair of government. [89]Floyd Hiatt Ross maintains that according to the Imperial Household Law that operated for many centuries, no emperor was truly emperor unless he possessed the sacred Treasures for the Shinto ceremony.

Ross asserts that people in younger generations who have grown up after the war know little about Shinto and the place that Shinto rituals played in the life of the emperor. Nevertheless, as far as the sentiment of the older generation was concerned, especially those who resided in the country and villages, the postwar legal changes meant little.

The imperial family still enjoys very high esteem and prestige among the nation's ruling class and leading Shinto

88   Wikipedia: Fujiwara clan. Online at http://en.wikipedia.org/wiki/Fujiwara_clan
89   Floyd Hiatt Ross. Shinto The Way of Japan. (Boston, USA: Beacon Press, 1965) p. 58

shrines remain important symbols of Japanese nationhood and closely integrated into daily life of the average Japanese citizens. Extreme and fanatic ultranationalists continued to view the emperor as god and treat him with a deep reverence and awe. Since the end of the Pacific War, the status of Yasukuni Shrine has been a matter of some controversy, because critics fear that it might foster a revival of Shinto led nationalism.

[90] Hayao Miyazaki. Princess Mononoke, 1997.[91]

---

90 Was available June 2010: http://animewotaku.cscblog.jp/img/A2-52.jpg
91 The picture is used under "fair dealing" (Canada) and "fair use" (USA) provisions in copyright law.

CHAPTER 3

SHINTO AS A CEREMONIAL RELIGION

Shinto has been Japan's public ceremonial religion with a rich variety of annual agricultural rites and other rituals to bring good luck and remove bad luck or omens, and has been associated with the imperial court from the Yamato era. [92]Ross (1965) states that Shinto has numerous festivals throughout a year from antiquity. He contends that:

> The festivals have been the main support of
> the life of Shinto and the priests have tried
> to keep the ritual as faithfully as possible.
> This is especially true of ancient shrines such
> as those at Izumo and Ise, but it also holds
> true at many other places (Ross, 1965)

Shinto rituals were deeply rooted in daily life of Japanese people and most of them were associated with harvest rites from the ancient times.

Taiho Codes of 701

[93]According to Ellwood and Pilgrim (1992), Shinto rites were standardized after the Taika Reform by Nakatomi no Kamatari (藤原鎌足) in 646 BC during the reign of Emperor Tenji (天智天皇). These rites followed the Taiho Codes of 701, stated in the foundational documents named Ritsuryo State. [94]The Taiho Code or Code of Taiho (大宝律令 Taihō-ritsuryō) was an

---

92   Floyd Hiatt Ross.Shinto The Way of Japan.(Boston, USA:Beacon Press,1965)
      p. 54
93   Robert S. Ellwood & Richard Pilgrim, Japanese religion (NJ: Prentice Hall, Inc,
      1992), pp. 133-134.
94   Wikipedia: Taihō Code. Online at http://en.wikipedia.org/wiki/Code_of_Taiho

administrative reorganization enacted in 701 in Japan at the end of the Asuka period. The code was compiled at the direction of Prince Osakabe (忍坂部皇子) (died 705), Fujiwara no Fuhito (藤原不比等) (659–720) and Awata no Mahito (粟田真人), at the request of Emperor Mommu (文武天皇) (683-707). Similar to many other developments in the country at the time, it was largely an adaptation of the governmental system of China's *Tang* Dynasty with some Korean influence as well.

The Taiho Code established two departments of government: the *Jingi-kan,* or Department of Worship and the *Daijō-kan,* or Department of State. The *Jingi-kan* was the higher branch, taking precedence over the Daijō-kan that handled all spiritual, religious and ritualistic matters. The *Jingi-kan* was responsible for annual festivals and official court ceremonies such as coronations, as well as the upkeep of shrines, discipline of shrine wardens, and recording and observation of oracles and divinations. The *Daijō-kan* handled all secular and administrative matters.

The Code provided for a court and administration based on Chinese models adapted to Japanese society pertaining to Shinto spirituality and the traditions of ancient houses, including the imperial house. This pattern of ceremonial Shinto, the *Taiho Codes* of 701 flourished in the Nara and Heian period.

[95]Koichi Mori (1979) contended that the *Taiho Codes* of 701 institutionalized the ritual of the imperial household as affairs of state and the main shrines throughout the country were placed under the direct control of the imperial court. Shinto shrines all over the country were also hierarchically placed under the Grand Shrine of Ise, the shrine dedicated to Sun Goddess Amaterasu.

Agricultural Rites

Many of the Shinto festivals were associated with the food supply because Japan had been an agricultural society since the Yayoi period. [96]Ellwood and Pilgrim (1992) discuss the way the major Shinto court rites in that time centered on two poles

---

95   Koichi Mori. The Emperor of Japan: A historical study in Religious Symbolism. Japanese journal of Religious Studies, 1979 p. 527
96   Robert S. Ellwood & Richard Pilgrim, Japanese religion (NJ: Prentice Hall, Inc, 1992)

- the Imperial Palace and the *Grand Shrine of Ise* (伊勢神宮) some 60 miles apart that both dealt with annual, calendarical, and typically agrarian festivities around the year. The principal rituals were the *Toshigoi* (祈年) or spring prayers for the crops at the palace, and *Niinamesai* (新嘗祭) or harvest festival in the fall performed by the emperor at the palace. These were rites to promote fertility and give thanksgiving to Kami, or gods who gracefully brought harvests. Ellwood and Pilgrim state that the significance of the ancient Japanese emperor's role in the harvest rites were closely allied with the role of archaic sacred ruler, or Priest King, whose major obligation was to magically bestow fertility. [97]

[98]Apart from rituals performed annually, there was another significant rite called *Daijosai* (大嘗祭) or Grand Food Festival of New Food at Ascension performed in connection with an emperor's ascension to the throne. After the death of the preceding emperor, the heir to the throne prepared himself for his new position in a sacred chamber of the imperial court where he ritually purified himself. During the rite, there were a few taboos including that the emperor-to-be did not expose himself to the sun because the sun would destroy the emperor-spirit.

[99]Middle Festivals included the festivals of praying for a good harvest early in February, monthly festivals, and the festival of the new rice crop. Shinto also had several lesser festivals that included festivals of praying for an abundant rice crop, soul-quieting ceremony, festival for appeasing the *Fire Kami*, a festival of the road Kami and festivals associated with particular shrines.

[100]Ross contends that there were five purposes expressed in the various types of rituals. They were:

1. Making requests to Kami for such things as sons, good rice crops and good health.

97   Mori. The Emperor of Japan: A historical study in Religious Symbolism., pp.134-135.
98   Mori. The Emperor of Japan: A historical study in Religious Symbolism. pp. 531
99   Floyd Hiatt Ross. Shinto The Way of Japan.(Boston,USA:Beacon Press,1965) 54
100   Floyd Hiatt Ross. Shinto The Way of Japan. (Boston, USA: Beacon Press, 1965) p. 58

2. Expression of thanks to Kami for benefits
   or graces already bestowed.
3. Pacifying or soothing Kami who might
   otherwise be violent or dangerous.
4. Magical festivals.
5. Festivals of divination.

According to Ross, these rites always had a very important place in the life of the peasants who were extremely vulnerable under the ruthless forces of the nature and therefore needed divine protection. He also maintains some rituals which belong to the first three categories belong to the imperial household. However, although he was the chief priest or a person who intervened with deities and performed the rites, he alone did not officiate these rituals, but the entire community was involved in the ceremony, according to [101]Ellwood and Pilgrim (1992).

Court rituals were not the sole prerogative of the emperor, just as local shrine rituals were not simply those of the priest but of the entire community. Also, several members of various prominent families played important roles in the rituals, holding traditional functions. Clans like the Soga, the Fujiwara, and the Nakatomi became part of Japanese ruling oligarchies in Japanese ancient histories.

Prior to the Meiji Restoration, the *Nakatomi* clan performed the [102]*Ise Grand Shrine* rituals. The clan of Wataari, the local priestly house, presented offerings to a god Toyouke at the outer shrine. The entire Shinto based court and ceremonial system was under the supervision of the court shrine administration branch. From the Yamato era, there was the system called "unitary sacro-society" or the system in which the court and religion became one and the emperor was also the high priest. However, their sole purpose was fertility, agricultural matters and the personal and social well being of each citizen throughout various events in life, or festivities in the routine of life cycle.

---

101   Robert S. Ellwood & Richard Pilgrim, Japanese religion (NJ: Prentice Hall, Inc, 1992)
102   The Grand Shrine of Ise was the place of a legend that Amaterasu, the Sun goddess descended from the sky.

Therefore, the ancient Shinto based ceremonial system was essentially different from the social psychological War God Machine created by Meiji Oligarchy in which the emperor was a sacred, inviolable demigod.

Dormancy of Imperial Power

As previously stated, there was a long period in which the emperor's power faded and was dormant or almost invisible in Japan's history. This political authority began to wane in the early ninth century. The real political power of the state was taken by Fujiwara Clan in the late twelfth century by the Samurai. The state of the emperor's dormancy continued until the Meiji Restoration in 1868. Nearly 1,000 years of Fujiwara Clan and Samurai rule made the emperor almost completely invisible from the public and political realm.

Even during this time, rulers of Japan retained the system of Taiho Code for court and administration so that the emperor was still technically head of the nation. According to [103]Tetsuro Watsuji (1889-1960), the emperor and his household seemed to have retained considerable respect and reverence as a high priest of the Shinto Religion.

[104]When US Admiral Matthew Perry[105] (1794-1858) demanded that Japan must open its door to foreign trade in 1852 as he visited Kurihama Japan, he thought Tokugawa Shogun was the king of Japan and did not realize there was another monarchy or the emperor there. [106]Tetsuro Watsuji (1962), however, contends that the reverence for the emperor appeared in literary works from the time of the ancient nation through the Tokugawa period.

---

103   Wikipedia: Tetsuro Watsuji. Online at http://en.wikipedia.org/wiki/Tetsuro_
      Watsuji
104   Mori. The Emperor of Japan: A historical study in Religious Symbolism. p. 526
105   Wikipedia: Matthew Calbraith Perry. Online at http://de.wikipedia.org/wiki/
      Matthew_Perry_(Offizier)
106   Tetsuro Watsuji. Sonno shiso to sono dento [Reverence for the emperor and
      its tradition]. In Watsuji Tetsuro Zenshu [Complete works of Watsuji Tetsuro].
      (Tokyo: Iwanami Shoten, 1962)

[107] The Grand Shrine of Ise, the center of
Shinto rites from the antiquity, 1997.[108]

---

107   Was available August 2010: http://k-kabegami.sakura.ne.jp/isejingu/open/19.
      html
108   The picture is used under "fair dealing" (Canada) and "fair use" (USA)
      provisions in copyright law.

CHAPTER 4

HISTORY OF THE YASUKUNI SHRINE

The Yasukuni Shrine today is considered the centre of Japan's nationalism exhibiting a somewhat biased view on the history of the Emperor Cult inherited from the State Shinto before the defeat of Japan in 1945. It has also been a stormy place as the source of numerous chronic controversies over the deification of war criminals, justification of Japan's military aggression to the neighbours in the East Asia and atrocities during several decades after the Second World War. Yasukuni, however, is a relatively recent shrine in comparison with the vast majority of the Shinto shrines including The Great Shrine of Ise in which Sun Goddess Amaterasu was enshrined as the central deity.

Humble Beginnings of Yasukuni

Yasukuni Shrine had a humble beginning as one of *Shokonsha*, or Shinto shrines built to honour and commemorate dead soldiers who fought against Tokugawa Shogun's government to accomplish the bourgeois revolution named the Meiji Restoration in 1868. The word *Shokonsha* (招魂社) had three components: *sho* "inviting," *Kon* "spirit" and *sha* "house." According to [109]D.C. Holtom (1963), it was a god-house into which the spirits of dead were summoned to take up residence, or into which they could be called under the mystic spell of various specific ceremonies.

Since Shinto god or *Kami* could be considered either historical or legendary persons, the first group of Yasukuni's *Kami* were souls of dead soldiers who fought for the Meiji

---

[109] D.C. Holtom, Modern Japan and Shinto Nationalism. (New York: USA Paragon Book Reprint Corp, 1963)

Restoration. From Christian point of view, enshrinement of dead persons as gods per se was a blasphemy and rebellion against the true God. But it was not a rebellion against God that might cause any socio-political disasters, for the sole purpose of the enshrinement was giving condolence to the war dead, not enhancement of nationalism, hostility and aggression against Japan's neighbours and enemies at all. In other words, the act of deifying dead soldiers was not yet linked to the nationalist ideology and formation of Kokutai, the socio-religious and social psychological system developed by the Meiji government. Yasukuni had the appearance of an ordinary Shinto Shrine when it came into the existence, and had no linkage with the notorious Japanese Nationalist or Emperor Cult.

Events Prior to Meiji Restoration

In the years of Tokugawa Shogunate rulership, there was a series of civil wars between the Tokugawa Shogun forces and what were called the Imperial Loyalists or [110]*Restorationists* who intended to defeat the Tokugawa Shogun Government and restore the emperor's power to the central position of the country, as it had been in the era prior to the tenth century. [111]William Daniel Sturgeon states that Loyalists from *Satsuma* and *Choshu* Provinces in Western Japan fought against the army of Tokugawa Shogunate and took over Kyoto in 1862. As the civil war in Japan progressed and more loyalist soldiers died, additional memorial services for the dead took place. [112]In December of the same year, 60 members of the Loyalist forces of *Tsuwano* clan gathered in Kyoto, Japan's capital in theTokugawa era to hold a memorial service called *Shokonsai*

---

110   They were called Restorationists because their goal was defeating the Tokugawa Shogun Government and established a new emperor centered government. During the Tokugawa era, the emperor existed as a figurehead. However, Shogun was the real authority and actual monarchy as well, British Writer Jonathan Swift described that Japan had two monarchies: Emperor and King (Shogun), in his popular novel "Gulliver's Travel." "Restoration" in this context meant to restore the original power and authority of the emperor, defeating the second monarchy or Shogun.

111   William Daniel Sturgeon, Japan's Yasukuni Shrine: Place of Peace or Place of Conflict? (Florida, USA: Dissertation.com, 1991) p. 29

112   Joshua Safier. Yasukuni Shrine and the Constraints on the Discourses of Nationalism in Twentieth-Century Japan. (Florida, USA: Dissertation.com, 1991) p. 22

(招魂祭) or "spirit inviting rite" for dead comrades who died in the battle against Shogun's army. They did it to give condolence to the soldiers who had died in battle for the loyalist cause since 1858.

As the memorial service took place, the leaders of the Loyalists army requested Emperor Komei (1831-1867), the immediate predecessor of Emperor Meiji, to officiate a memorial service for their dead comrades. Komei, known as a conservative among emperors in the Tokugawa era, generally agreed with the anti-Western sentiments of the Meiji Restorationists and began to take an active role in matters of state to sponsor a Shinto style memorial rite for the soldiers who died on the Emperor's behalf. As the battles and wars progressed, few additional memorial services were performed as the number of dead soldiers increased. Many "Shokonsha" or "houses to invite spirits of the deceased" were built continuously in different regions in Japan, until the series of civil wars were eventually over and the Meiji Restoration revolution that they intended was finally accomplished.

The final battle between the Tokugawa Shogunate and the Meiji Restorationists was called [113]Boshin War or *Boshin Senso* (戊辰戦争), "War of the Year of the Dragon" and took place in 1868. Around 120,000 men were mobilized during the conflict, and of these about 3,500 were killed. In February 1868, [114]Saigo Takamori (西郷隆盛) (1827 - 1877), the real life model of Katsumoto in the movie *The Last Samurai*, led the victorious imperial forces north and east through Japan, winning the *Battle of Kōshū-Katsunuma*. He eventually surrounded Edo in May 1868, leading to its unconditional surrender by Admiral [115]Katsu Kaishu (勝海舟) (1823 - 1899), the shogun's navy minister. Some groups continued to resist after this surrender but were defeated in the Battle of Ueno. Due to the persistence of Saigo Takamori, a prominent leader of the imperial faction, the Tokugawa loyalists were shown clemency, and many former

---

113   Wikepedia: Boshin War. Online at http://en.wikipedia.org/wiki/Boshin_War
114   Wikepedia: Saigo Takamori. Online at http://en.wikipedia.org/wiki/Saigo_
       Takamori
115   Wikepedia: Katsu Kaishū. Online at http://en.wikipedia.org/wiki/Katsu_Kaishu

Shogunate leaders including Admiral Katsu were later given positions of responsibility under the new government. Some groups, however, continued to resist after this surrender but were defeated in the Battle of Ueno.

Admiral [116]Enomoto Takeaki (榎本武揚) (1836 - 1908), one of leaders of the Shogun's navy, refused to surrender all of his ships. He remitted just four ships, but then escaped to Hokkaido in Japan's north with the remnants of the navy ships and 2,000 members of the navy in the hope of staging a counter-attack together with the northern daimyo. He was accompanied by a handful of French military advisers, including [117]Jules Brunet (1838 - 1911) a French officer who was sent to the Empire of Japan in order to help modernize the armies of the shogunate played an active role there. Jules had formally resigned from the French Army in order to accompany the rebels after the Shogun forces officially surrendered. As a Western military officer who sided a rebellion of a Japanese Samurai leader, Jules Brunet is believed partly the inspiration for the character of Nathan Algren in the 2003 movie *The Last Samurai*. Enomoto and his followers hoped to found a state under the rule of the Tokugawa family in Hokkaido, but the Meiji government refused their request. On December 25, they declared the foundation of the *Republic of Ezo* and elected Enomoto as president.

After the surrender of Shogun [118]Tokugawa Yoshinobu (徳川慶喜) (1837 – 1913), most of Japan accepted the emperor's rule. However, members of [119]*Byakkotai* (白虎隊) "White Tiger Corps," the diehard shogunate supporters in the North, continued the resistance. They were a group of more than 300 young, predominantly teenaged, samurai who belonged to the Aizu clan. On October 26, Edo was renamed Tokyo, and the Meiji era officially started. After a protracted month-long battle, Aizu finally admitted defeat on November 6, leading to the mass

116   Wikepedia: Enomoto Takeaki. Online at http://en.wikipedia.org/wiki/Enomoto_Takeaki
117   Wikepedia: Jules Brunet. Online at http://en.wikipedia.org/wiki/Jules_Brunet
118   Wikepedia: Tokugawa Yoshinobu. Online at http://en.wikipedia.org/wiki/Tokugawa_Yoshinobu
119   Wikepedia: Byakkotai. Online at http://en.wikipedia.org/wiki/Byakko-tai

suicide of the *Byakkotai* young warriors. Nineteen members committed *seppuku* on a hillside overlooking the Aizu Castle after the defeat of the rebellion in 1869.

Enomoto's navy joined the coalition led by the Aizu clan. Then, after the failure of their rebellion, the Meiji Governmental Army and Navy invaded Hokkaido and defeated the former Shogunate Army, as well as the Navy of the Republic in the Naval Battle of Hakodate. They also imprisoned President Enomoto of the republic and accused him of high treason, but in 1872 the new Meiji government pardoned him, since he was an extremely talented and useful person for the government. He rose astonishingly fast within the new ruling clique, faster and higher than any other member of the former Tokugawa clan. Enomoto was to become one of the few former Tokugawa retainers who could exert political influence in Meiji Japan as well, since the anti-Tokugawa clans from Choshu and Satsuma dominated politics in those days. In 1874, Enomoto was appointed vice-admiral, and, as a special envoy, he was sent to Russia to negotiate the Treaty of Saint Petersburg (1875), which was signed in the following year. In 1880, Enomoto rose to Navy Minister (海軍卿) of the Imperial Japanese Navy because of his many political and diplomatic accomplishments.

Enomoto successively held several ministry positions in the government and played an active role in promoting Japanese imperialistic expansionism through settler colonies in the Pacific Ocean and South and Central America. He was successful in his career after the rebellion failed, yielded his cause and complied with the rulers of the Meiji government.

However, many Japanese regarded him as an opportunist with no sense of consistency who disregarded the traditional Samurai class code of honour, since he became a loyal dog of the Meiji oligarchy after the rebellion failed. Also, men who obeyed his order to fight against the Meiji restorationist forces and died during the rebellion led by Saigo were labelled as the enemies of the emperor forever.

Souls of the dead who sided the shogunate forces like *labelled* warriors and officers who followed and died in the battle were excluded from Yasukuni, since the shrine was built for the Imperial loyalists. Nevertheless, the primary impetus for doing the succession of ceremonies during the era of civil wars was to give condolence to dead soldiers who came from nothing more than the respect to deceased comrades who died in the battle. [120]However, Joshua Safer, who wrote a master's thesis on the Yasukuni history, observed the initial development of the cultic State Shinto and the intentionality to press Shinto based nationalism among those loyalists holding the ceremony. He states that:

> The primary impetus for those ceremonies grew out of respect for fallen comrades and human compassion. They were also reflection of Restoration Shinto. During the Tokugawa period the dead had been buried according to Buddhist ritual. However, to leaders of the restoration movement, Buddhism was perceived as corrupting foreign influence incompatible with the Japanese spirit (Safer, 1990).

Those Shinto restorationists attempted to exclude any foreign religions signs as corruption and pursued the pure form of Shinto holding to the myth that the emperor was a Kami descended from the sun-goddess Amaterasu. In fact, there was no such thing as pure and uncontaminated form of Shinto even from the Yamato or Yayoi era. Shinto religion had an extremely long history of concretisation with Taoism, Confucianism and Buddhism from prehistory. But those who advocated Shinto restorationism built their ideology based on myth instead of historical data. It is ironic that Shinto restorationists who pursued the pure form of Shinto incorporated the philosophy of the Enlightenment from the West into their belief system and created the cult named State Shinto.

---

120   Joshua Safier. Yasukuni Shrine and the Constraints on the Discourses of Nationalism in Twentieth-Century Japan. (Florida, USA: Dissertation.com, 1991) p. 23

Meiji Government & Development of Yasukuni Cult

Under the Meiji government, *Shokonsha* were constructed in all of 52 new prefectures, putting monuments of Japan's war dead throughout the nation. The purpose of building new Shokonsha all over the country was not merely to commemorate dead soldiers, but to establish the foundation of the militaristic ideology of the Meiji Government and newly developed Emperor Cult. Among them, there was the Tokyo Shokonsha built in 1869. Under the new government with emperor-centered nationalist ideology, Tokyo Shokonsha became the main shrine among all shrines built for war dead and then was renamed Yasukuni Shrine by Emperor Meiji (明治天皇) in 1879.

Since then, Yasukuni Shrine or *Yasukuni Jinja* (靖国神社), that literally means to be a Peaceful Country Shrine, demonstrated an extremely peculiar view of the peace during centuries from the Meiji era, and became the iconographic centre of Japanese ultra-nationalism. Regarding Yasukuni's secondary role to enhance Japan's ultra-nationalism, [121]William Daniel Sturgeon contends that although the Yasukuni Shrine served primarily the religious role to commemorate war dead, especially during its early years, it later took on another role with less religious purpose. It became the national epicenter of state-rites for dead soldiers.

After the Meiji Restoration, Yasukuni was gradually transformed into the centre to impose Kokutai or State Supported Emperor Cult to the Japanese public. In other words, it was becoming a ceremonial site to enhance and worship an emperor centered ideological system from a place originally built simply to honour and give condolence to the war dead. From the beginning of the 20th century, particularly during the time of the Second World War, Yasukuni's primary role was the enhancement of Japan's ultra-nationalism or a massive dose of a social psychological steroid or Viagra to the whole nation. This was because all other objectives were becoming less important for the military-led government controlled by extremely fanatic

---

121   William Daniel Sturgeon, Japan's Yasukuni Shrine: Place of Peace or Place of Conflict? (Dissertations.com, 2006) p. 36

followers of the emperor cult that was the core of the State Shinto and Kokutai.

Leaders of the Meiji Government was engineered to modify the spirituality and praxis of Shinto and 1,700 year old state governing system created by Prince Shotoku into a kind of "black box" or device to attempt to deceive their citizens and produce blind followers of the leaders and polity under the Meiji Emperor. [122]Helen Hardcre (1989) contends that during the early Meiji era, worship at Shinto Shrines throughout Japan was coordinated with the Imperial worship calendar as well as the Grand Shrine of Ise. Her conclusion is that the nationwide orchestration of rituals was an attempt of "daring social engineering." Meiji government used this engineered Nationalist Shinto system to unify the people in a single cult, headed by the emperor as the chief priest. The entire spiritual system they created was a very clever mechanism to bolster the concept of the semi-divine emperor as the head of the state.

Since then, engineered Shinto deviated from original simple animistic spirituality, and became like a gigantic, horrendous and formidable monster which harmed Japan's own citizens and neighbours like God Warriors in Nausicaä of the Valley of the Wind," (1984) by Hayao Miyazaki.[123] The story is set thousands of years in the future following a deadly war and the ensuing an ecological holocaust that has destroyed most of the Earth and wiped out almost all of humanity. The destruction occurs during the now-legendary Seven Days of Fire when monsters named God Warriors destroyed the entire human civilization. They are biomechanical creatures created by the modern genetic engineering technology.[124] In the same way, a monster called State Shinto kept on growing and feeding on the blood of Japanese Imperial soldiers as well as ordinary citizens, including neighbours like China and Korea right until Japan's final defeat and surrender in 1945.

---

122   Helen Hardcre, Shinto and the State. (Princeton: Princeton University Press, 1989)

123   Hayao Miyazaki Web, 2006. Online at http://www.nausicaa.net/miyazaki/

124   Wikipedia: Nausicaä of the Valley of the Wind (film). Online at http://en.wikipedia.org/wiki/Nausica%C3%A4_of_the_Valley_of_the_Wind_(film)

Yasukuni Shrine began as a humble beginning as a site to commemorate dead soldiers, however it turned into the centre of bloody diabolic cult that somehow resembled with a monster *Kaonashi* or "no face" in another Miyazaki animation movie [125]*Spirited Away*. As Yasukuni fed more soldiers' flesh and blood, the monstrous spirituality grew larger and more unmanageable. *Kaonashi* was originally a shy, harmless and quiet humanoid without face in his first appearance in the movie and not a destructive monster like *God Warrior* at all. But once he was fed a negative energy, he turned into a gluttonous and horrendous man-eater like Yasukuni Shrine's Kami.

Also, once he started eating people, Kaonashi was not able to stop man-eating like Yasukuni Shrine. *Kaonashi* kept on eating people and continued to grow like Yasukuni's evil spirits until *Sen,* the main character of the movie, gave him the remainder of the herbal cake, which caused him to regurgitate the food and three people he had eaten. His gluttony was cured once he followed *Sen* outside and threw up all he ate. Likewise, the gluttony of Yasukuni's Kami finally ceased when the Imperial Japan was defeated and the State Shinto and Kokutai were dismantled.

---

125   Wikipedia: Spirited Away. Online at http://en.wikipedia.org/wiki/Spirited_Away

[126]Hayao Miyazaki. Nausicaä of the Valley of the Wind, 1984.[127]

---

126   Was available June 2010; http://little-writing.blogspot.com/2007/08/blog-post_179.html

127   The picture is used under "fair dealing" (Canada) and "fair use" (USA) provisions in copyright law.

CHAPTER 5

YASUKUNI SHRINE,
SHINTO *JIHAD* & EMPEROR CULT

Meiji Restoration and State Shinto

During the Meiji period, the Japanese imperial government systematized traditional Shinto teachings and rites as State Shinto and used it for legitimizing the imperial regime and securing the people's loyalty to the emperor. The emperor was regarded as the living god who was a descendant of the great Sun Goddess *Amaterasu*; therefore dying for the emperor was a glorified act pertaining to the greatest honor for the Japanese.

This State Shinto, which was closely associated with the emperor system and militarism, had a clear distinction from the primordial Shinto, or primitive and more benign counterpart. If animistic and primitive Shinto were classified as naturally brewed Shinto, the State Shinto represented by Yasukuni Shrine was a mutated or genetically altered one with bio-engineering technology by the leaders of Meiji government.

Regarding the role of emperor system after the Meiji Restoration (明治維新), [128]Koichi Mori (1979), maintains that it served as the key principle of social and political unification from the very beginning of the Meiji period and most scholars of modern Japanese history agreed with this. Freed from the authority of Tokugawa Shogunate, Meiji Restoration leaders chose to employ an emperor-system as the principle by which to rule the nation and increase the economic and military strength of the nation-state. The leaders of the Meiji government incorporated the emperor system into a newly developed State Shinto and

---

128   Mori. The Emperor of Japan: A historical study in Religious Symbolism. p. 522

built the foundation of a totalitarian state. Mori argues that they employed the emperor system to rule the nation because the power of the emperor as a religious symbol was convenient for them. Before the Meiji Restoration, the emperor was respected by Japanese people as the most central mythological figure in their popular memory, although he had politically no power. So the attitude of the people toward the emperor was an important element in the structure of Japanese collective psychology and belief system.

Mori (1979) also maintains that the fact that the Shinto believed that the emperor descended from Sun Goddess Amaterasu was a very significant foundational story for the typically agrarian Japanese people. The emperor was the high priest who performed rice-crop rituals, and for the majority of Japanese people made their life as farmers and rice was the most essential part of their life. Farmers' life in antiquity relied on the shamanic power of the emperor or his well being as the agricultural priest who performed rites for the fertility. In the time of the Meiji restoration, the emperor's role as a shaman who performed fertility rituals for their remote ancestors still remained in the popular memory of people or collective subconscious among Japanese. Meiji restorationists exploited this very archaic memory or foundational story of the agrarian nation in which the emperor was the high priest who performed the agricultural rites and nurtured the whole nation, to construct Emperor Cult, which required a blind submission of all citizens of Japan to the authority. The emperor as the agricultural high priest was long remembered by Japanese people as an icon who saved the farmers' life from famines and other natural disasters through the rites of magic or active interventions with the spiritual forces that he performed.

[129]So until the time the Meiji Restoration took place in 1868, Japan was still a fundamentally agricultural society and the emperor was a religious symbol of Japan's agrarian communities. Therefore the Meiji government tried to use the emperor as a driving force to transform agrarian Japan into

---

129   Mori. The Emperor of Japan: A historical study in Religious Symbolism. p. 547

an industrious, capitalist nation-state with a strong military so that she could compete with empires in the West. It was a unconventional and utilitarian method to utilize the emperor as a religious icon of agrarian community to "deagriculturate" the nation. Mori (1979) states that the goal of the government was the "creation of a rich country with a strong military." As *Omura* in the movie *the Last Samurai* exhibited, the means of modernization of the country during the Meiji era was the utilisation of Western science and technology. This demonstrated that the Meiji government wanted to employ a strong ideology that might drive the people to devote their energy to construct a powerful, formidable nation-state. The ideology they employed, according to Mori, was *kazoku kokka* or the state as a family or household. The imperial family, then, was deemed the head of all families in Japan.

In order to promote the emperor-centered ethical values of loyalty and filial piety in the nation wide scale, the government stipulated the emperor's sacredness, inviolability, and the unbroken continuity of his divine lineages from antiquity in a constitution made public in 1889. [130]From Article 1-3, the Meiji Constitution was founded on the principle that sovereignty resided in the person of the Emperor by virtue of his divine ancestry "unbroken for ages eternal," rather than in the people. Article 4 stated that the "Emperor was the head of the Empire, combining in Himself the rights of sovereignty." Meiji Constitution, promulgated by Emperor Meiji on 11 February 1889, came into effect on 29 November 1890. The first Imperial Diet, a new representative assembly, convened on the day the Meiji Constitution came into force.

In 1890, the Meiji Government also enacted the [131]*Imperial Rescript on Education* in the name of the emperor. The Rescript emphasized the Confucian virtues of loyalty and filial piety as well as the sacredness of the emperor. It promoted public good common interests; respect for the Constitution and observation

---

130   Wikipedia: Meiji Constitution. Online at http://en.wikipedia.org/wiki/Meiji_
       Constitution
131   Wikipedia: Imperial Prescript on Education. Online at http://en.wikipedia.org/
       wiki/Imperial_Rescript_on_Education

of its laws. It also asked citizens that "should an emergency arise, offer yourselves courageously to the State; and thus guard and maintain the prosperity of Our Imperial Throne coeval with heaven and earth." [132]In 1891, the government distributed to each school a copy of the Imperial Rescript on Education, a photograph of Emperor Meiji, and another photograph of the empress. All public and private schools in Japan were required to display the pictures and read the Rescript on stated occasions. They were also instructed to incorporate the content of the Rescript into their curriculum of moral and ethical education.

[133]From this Meiji Restoration up until the defeat in the Pacific War in 1945, the Shinto religion was focused sharply on Ise Shrine and Yasukuni Shrine. The Meiji Government invented elaborate imperial myths around the Emperor, and an ideological system called *Kokutai* or a "moral concept that constituted the very essence of the state." *Kokutai* was a form of unitary sacro-society or nation-wide totalitarian spiritual community, in which the Emperor and his inviolability as centre of the cult was propagated in the popular mind through education, politics and social values. [134]Joshua Safier (1991) contends that the emperor ideology was predicated upon the people's unconditional and unlimited responsibility for protecting this system and the sacredness of the Emperor himself. Also Daikichi Irokawa (1985) views the emperor system as an enormous black box that people could not see the inside, or were not even allowed to raise questions about. Irokawa states that:

> [135]The emperor system as a way of thinking was like an enormous black box into which the whole nation, intellectuals as well as commoners, unknowingly walked. Once within its confines, the comers of the box obscured in the darkness,

132   Mori. The Emperor of Japan: A historical study in Religious Symbolism. pp. 548-49
133   Mori. The Emperor of Japan: A historical study in Religious Symbolism. 1979 p. 527
134   Joshua Safier, Yasukuni Shrine and the Constraints on the Discourses of Nationalism in Twentieth-Century Japan. (Dissertation.com, 1991), p. 29
135   Irokawa Daikichi. The Culture of Meiji Period. (Princeton: Princeton University Press, 1985) p. 245.

the people were unable to see what it was that
hemmed them in. The emperor system became part
of the landscape; disappearing into the Japanese
environment until the people throught it was a
product of their own village community, rather
than a system of control above (Irokawa, 1985).

In other words, the system that Meiji government created
was a gigantic Hologram or artificially made reality or illusion
based on the myth in which the emperor was a divine and all
powerful being descended from above. It employed the same
technique as contemporary cult leaders to control followers.
From the Meiji Restoration to the end of the Pacific War, the
entire nation state of Japan was a cult organisation in which the
emperor was divine and inviolable and all citizens or subjects
were demanded to have blind faith and not allowed to raise any
questions.

Within the newly developed imperial cult by the Meiji
Government, Yasukuni Shrine assumed the role of contributor
to the psychological appeal of the Emperor's divinity.
Enshrinements were ordered by the Emperor, and he visited
Yasukuni more frequently than any other shrine except for the
Grand Shrine of Ise. The Meiji Emperor paid tribute at Yasukuni
seven times, the Taisho Emperor twice, and prior to Japan's
surrender in 1945, Showa Emperor (Hirohito) visited the shrine
20 times. The Emperor always appeared in military costume
and acted as the Supreme Commander of Japanese Army and
Navy. Each death of a soldier in his name fortified spiritual and
psychological components of nationalism, ethnocentrisms, and
emperor-centred worldview among the citizens.

According to [136]David M. O'Brien and Yasuo Ohsaki
(1996), prior to World War II, State Shinto, which centered
on the worship of the emperor and Yasukuni Shrine's cult of
war dead, were established in support of the government and
militarism. O'Brien and Ohsaki indicated that the State Shinto

---

136   David M O'Brien and Yasuo Ohsaki. To dream of dreams: religious freedom and
      constitutional politics in postwar Japan. (Honolulu : University of Hawaii Press,
      c1996)

created by the Meiji government had very unique and peculiar characteristics. The authors focused on the people struggling against the government attempts to revive "the emperor system" and Japan's prewar military presence with the strong connection to the State Shinto.

[137]O'Brien and Ohsaki maintains that the Emperor System and State Shinto rested on a profound paradox. While the emperor was venerated as "the son of the heaven," an all-powerful embodiment of the unity of Shinto and the State, he was in fact constitutionally constrained. Under the Meiji Constitution, the emperor was reigning, but did not possess a de facto ruling power. The Emperor Meiji (明治天皇) (1868-1912) actively questioned his ministers and the government leaders in his court, and therefore influenced their decision-making. However, the Emperor himself made only a few decisions, only when ministerial advisors were divided. Meiji's grandson, Hirohito (裕仁) (1900-1989) also actively questioned his ministers during his long reign, yet he too rarely directly asserted independent judgment except at the very end of World War II.

[138]The authors describe how religious minorities including Christians have sought the enforcement of provisions for the free exercise of religion. Kanzo Uchimura (内村鑑三) (1861-1930), a great evangelist and the founder of the "Non-Church" Christian Movement was censured for refusing to pay homage to the Imperial Prescript of Education while he was a high school teacher. O'Brien and Ohsaki maintain that after the Russo-Japanese War (1904-1905), State Shinto gradually became more pervasive and suppressed the freedom of religion. It became increasingly aggressive, oppressive, forceful and exceptionally evil to the point in which its religiosity might be classified as demonic.

Japan's State Shinto was a social entity which continued to feed on soldiers' souls and grew. The number of enshrinements

---

137   O'Brien and Ohsaki. To dream of dreams : religious freedom and constitutional politics in postwar Japan, p. 42
138   O'Brien and Ohsaki. To dream of dreams : religious freedom and constitutional politics in postwar Japan, p. 43

grew incrementally after the Sino-Japanese War (1894-1895), Russo-Japanese War (1904-1905) and annexation of Korea in 1910, and the subsequent colonization of China. In addition the Great Meiji Shrine was constructed in Tokyo (1915-1926), and became the centre of the Emperor Worship cult along with Yasukuni. It was a national monument of the late Great Emperor Meiji, enshrining both the emperor and empress as gods.

[139]As the numbers of dead soldiers increased, State Shinto captured people's imagination, and vigorously imposed itself throughout the country. In their classrooms, Japanese grade school students were instructed that soldiers dying for their country, and the emperor, would earn deification and the highest honor. Schools encouraged their pupils to join the army or navy, fight for the emperor, die with highest honor, and be successfully enshrined as gods in Yasukuni Shrine. During these days, many Japanese believed that dedicating their entire life to the emperor, or living *Kami*, and dying for him with honor, was the ultimate goal or *raison d'etre* of life.

Japan's culture several years prior to World War II somewhat resembled the [140]*Klingons* in the fictional *Star Trek* universe or possibly worse. The Klingons who followed *Way of the Warrior*, the belief and value system developed by the legendary [141]*Emperor Kahless* show a resemblance to pre-World War II Japanese. Those who die with purpose and honor are said to join Kahless, who had been the first Klingon emperor, and a messianic figure in the Way of the Warrior. One could speculate that the *Star Trek* producers used Japanese militarism as the model of Klingons and Kahless was modeled after [142]*Jimmu*, the legendary divine warrior emperor from Kojiki and Nihonshoki. The same kind of cult-like approach as Pre Second World War Japan and the Klingons can also be said to be found among the Islamic nations in the Middle East and terrorist organizations

---

139   O'Brien and Ohsaki. To dream of dreams : religious freedom and constitutional politics in postwar Japan, pp. 44-45
140   Wikipedia: Klingon culture. Online at http://en.wikipedia.org/wiki/Klingon_culture
141   Wikipedia: Kahless. Online at http://en.wikipedia.org/wiki/Kahless
142   Wikipedia: Emperor Jimmu. Online at http://en.wikipedia.org/wiki/Emperor_Jimmu

following the cause of Islam today. In an episode of the [143]*Star Trek: The Next Generation* a clone of Kahless becomes emperor of the Klingon Empire. The clone emperor of the Klingons was a figurehead, with power residing with the Klingon High Council in the same way as the Meiji Emperor.

Religious Organization Law under Kichiro Hiranuma

[144]In 1940, the government of Japan under Prime Minister [145]Kiichiro Hiranuma (平沼　騏一郎) (1867–1952) enacted the notorious *Religious Organization Law*. Under this law, the government was able to control all religious matter of every regulating religious organization as it did all corporations. Religious organizations had to apply for and be granted government recognition to operate legally. The recognition depended on the religious body's agreement with the teaching and rites and support of the emperor's divinity. Many pastors did comply with the government's demand and participated in the rituals of Shinto Shrine. They defended their actions as participation in the "Shinto style non religious rituals." Some of them went so far as to incorporate the Imperial Rescript on Education into their sermons.

[146]During World War II, Christians and other religious minorities were ruthlessly persecuted both in Japan and her colonies in Asia for refusing to profess the emperor's divinity. Tadao Yanaihara (1893-1961), an outspoken Christian academic, and a leader of the Non-Church Christian Movement who apprenticed under Uchimura, was driven from his teaching position at Tokyo University in 1937. In Yokohama, seven Catholic priests were shot to death by fanatic ultra-nationalists

---

143   Wikipedia: Star Trek: The Next Generation. Online at http://en.wikipedia.org/ wiki/Star_Trek:_The_Next_Generation

144   O'Brien and Ohsaki. To dream of dreams : religious freedom and constitutional politics in postwar Japan, p. 46

145   Kiichiro Hiranuma was one of 14 convicted Class-A War criminal. He died in prison in 1952, was enshrined as *Kami* in Yasukuni Shrine. Hiranuma's deeds were even more evil than 7 of them who were sentenced to death and hanged in 1948. (In my personal opinion, Prime Minister Tojo who was hanged in 1948 was much better person than Hiranuma). Yet surprisingly, he was sentenced to life imprisonment instead.

146   O'Brien and Ohsaki. To dream of dreams : religious freedom and constitutional politics in postwar Japan, p. 45

or Emperor Cult followers. In June 1942, more than 100 pastors of the United Church of Christ of Japan (日本基督教団) were arrested on the charge of disturbing the peace. During their trials, their faith was tested as the prosecutors asked them, "Who do you think is greater, the Emperor or the Christ?" They were imposed an alternative between the sin of blasphemy by affirming the former, or imprisonment by maintaining allegiance to the latter. Many ministers died in prison, while others yielded to the imposition of evil gods upon them, or left the country.

[147]O'Brien and Ohsaki maintain that the [148]Meiji Constitution rejected establishment of any religion supported by the State and extensively guaranteed religious freedom. Yet, Japan's State Shinto continued to grow and became increasingly oppressive until the end of the Second World War. The persecution extended to many religious organizations including well established Buddhists and even some Shinto sects who did not practice Emperor Worship. In the Diet, Prime Minister Kiichiro Hiranuma made a stunning statement that, "In our country the way of the *Kami* is the absolute way, and teachings which differ from this and conflict with it are not allowed to exist."

Hiranuma was the prime minister of Japan from January 5 to August 30, 1939. As a defender of State Shintoism, he organized the "Shintoist Rites Research Council" based on the superiority of Shinto faith to all other faiths and the legitimacy of the *Religious Organization Law*. He then ruthlessly persecuted opponents of the State Shinto and the pathological political ideology. He could be viewed as the most evil prime minister Japan ever had, as he supported an aggressive military policy in China and envisioned expansion of the Great Japanese Empire to the whole of East Asia. Hiranuma eventually provoked war against the United States and Britain by signing an alliance with Germany, shortly before being replaced by [149]Prince Fumimaro

---

147   O'Brien and Ohsaki. To dream of dreams : religious freedom and constitutional politics in postwar Japan, p. 46
148   Although Meiji constitution stipulated emperor's sacred or divine attribute, it didn't institutionalize State Shinto. However, leaders of the government went further and establish the State Shinto and very creepy *Emperor Cult*.
149   Wikipedia: Fumimaro Konoe. Online at http://en.wikipedia.org/wiki/Fumimaro_ Konoe

Konoe (1891–1945). Konoe, with better common sense than Hiranuma, tried to avoid the commencement of the war against the United States, however his efforts were futile. After Konoe resigned, General [150]Hideki Tojo (1884–1948) became the prime minister of Japan and commenced the war against the Allied Force including the United States and Britain.

[151]In the summer of 1945, when Japan's defeat in the war was apparent and Emperor Hirohito and the nation's leaders made the decision to accept the *Potsdam Declaration*, or an offer to accept an unconditional surrender to the Allied Force. Hiranuma, then chair of the Privy Council, confronted the emperor with his responsibility for the defeat that required him to apologize to the heroic spirits of the imperial founder of his house and other imperial ancestors. Hiranuma was correct that the emperor had responsibility for Japan's defeat. According to the logic of ordinary people, however, the emperor owed apology to the dead soldiers who sacrificed their lives to the country in his name and soldiers and civilians who were still alive and suffering for the loss – not the spirits of the ancestors. According to the perception of the average person, Hiranuma did not possess sanity and the clear perception of reality at the end of his political career, for his sense of priorities and hierarchy of important matters were totally distorted. Hiranuma's cognitive process was far apart and completely incomprehensible to the general population in and those outside of Japan.

Like [152]Osama bin Laden (born in 1957) and [153]Shoko Asahara (born in 1955) who gave his followers orders to attack the Tokyo Subway by [154]Sarin nerve gas (1995) and commit ruthless murders, Hiranuma was most likely a person without an ordinary person's conscience. Therefore, he had no hesitation to kill or imprison those who did not agree with the Emperor

---

150   Wikipedia: Hideki Tojo. Online at http://en.wikipedia.org/wiki/Hideki_Tojo
151   Herbert P. Bix Hirohito and the Making of Modern Japan p. 482
152   Wikipedia: Osama bin Laden. Online at http://en.wikipedia.org/wiki/Osama_bin_Laden
153   Wikipedia: Shoko Asahara. Online at http://en.wikipedia.org/wiki/Shoko_Asahara
154   Wikipedia: Sarin gas attack on the Tokyo subway. Online at http://en.wikipedia.org/wiki/Sarin_gas_attack_on_the_Tokyo_subway

Cult and dared to do all kinds of evils in order to promote his own religious and political propaganda in the name of the divine emperor descended from the sun-goddess Amaterasu. When Hiranuma was the prime minister, State Shinto had grown into a gigantic psycho-spiritual entity and sociological life form that acted in its own will and everyone in the country including its creators failed to control it at the end. Hiranuma was not the master, but a faithful servant of this beast who dared to sacrifice anything he wanted.

State Shinto in Hiranuma's time was nearly as destructive as the [155]*God Warriors* or *Kyojinhei* (巨神兵) in [156] *Nausicaä of the Valley of the Wind*, (1984) one of Hayao Miyazaki's best animation movies. They were monsters created by the biotechnology with great powers in the future world that destroyed the entire human civilization in seven days. Miyazaki's story took place 1,000 years after the war called "Seven Days of Fire." Bioengineered weapons in the future world, the giant God Warriors, completely burned down the earth and destroyed the ecosystem of the planet as well as the entire human civilization. Ruins and poisonous forests covered the earth, and the remaining humans have only retained fragments of the technologies from previous age. After the destruction, people lived in a world much like the Medieval Age.

Miyazaki's story eloquently speaks of the rulers on earth who have created extremely powerful and destructive weapons or political systems without the knowledge of the deadliness until they finally brought destruction. The creators would not know how diabolical the power of their creations was and would be astonished with the deadly power once the monsters were activated. Like Miyazaki's *God Warriors*, Japan's State Shinto had extremely problematic power. The Meiji Government also created another seeming monster named *Kokutai*, which was State Shinto's inseparable counterpart like a Siamese twin.

---

155   In some English Translation, *Kyojinhei* 巨神兵 was God Soldiers instead of God Warriors.

156   Hayao Miyazaki Web, 2006. Online at http://www.nausicaa.net/miyazaki/

The State Shinto and Kokutai, the problematic Siamese twin created by the Meiji Government, made the whole archipelago into a totalitarian state or a gigantic prison camp in which every single individual in the country was required to give blind submission to the government, total dedication to the state and sacrifice to the emperor, sometimes including their life. Yasukuni Shrine was the centre of State Shinto, Kokutai and Emperor Cult in which completely brainwashed youngsters vowed *Jihad* for the emperor to sacrifice their lives in order to defeat their enemies. Prior to the final departure with planes like *Zero Fighter*, *Suisei* and *Ohka* or *Kaiten*, the human torpedoes for the Kamikaze Mission, they had the last meal with their comrades, toasting glasses of sake and greeting each other by saying, [157]"See you later in Yasukuni." They expected to get together in Yasukuni as Kami and feast again after the accomplishment of the mission and successful deification after dying for the Emperor.

Slanted View of Japan's Military History

Yasukuni Shrine's history museum contains an account of Japan's actions in that war, which many considered revisionist. [158]Shrine officials denied the legitimacy of the Tokyo War Trial and maintained that those 14 convicted criminals were "martyrs" who gave up their lives after the end of the Great East Asian War (Asian segment of the Second World War), taking upon themselves the responsibility for the war.

The shrine named the 1,068, "Martyrs of Showa" - those who died in the war including those 12 *Convicted Class-A War Criminals* and another two who were prosecuted as *War Criminals* but died before the verdicts came. The shrine ignited the rage of many in China and Korea as they learned that those 14 had been named Class-A War Criminals by the Allied Force tribunal. Yasukuni Shrine continued to profess that they were cruelly and unjustly tried as war criminals by a sham-like tribunal.

---

157   Gerald Hanley. See you in Yasukuni (New York: World Pub. Co., 1969/1970)
158   Welcome to Yasukuni's Home Page. Online at http://www.yasukuni.or.jp/english/

Yushukan War Memorabilia Museum

Yushukan War Memorabilia Museum, the shrine's history museum, originally built in 1882, became an integral part of Yasukuni Shrine. [159]John Breen (2004) described the Yushukan as "an integral component of the shrine complex and participants in the autumn and spring rites were actively encouraged to visit." Breen saw the Yushukan as a museum for *Kami* or deities of Shinto belief system, not simply a museum about the shrine. One of objectives the Yushukan's was to honour and comfort the Kami enshrined in the Yasukuni. All artefacts and displays belonged to Kami, being used as tools to comfort and pacify them. If the museum had only objective to pacify the dead soldiers it doesn't affect anyone except *Kami* or souls enshrined as gods. However, the museum had the second objective to demonstrate and propagate the Yasukuni's nationalist worldview and Shinto based ideology and political propaganda. This second objective made the museum one of the most malignant factors of the shrine, which might be used to poison the entire Japanese public and impact international community.

The Yushukan was once ordered to close in the postwar era by American occupational forces because it was the centre propagated Japanese militarism, ultranationalism and distorted worldview, but reopened in 1961. After reopened, the museum continued to exhibit a specific worldview and historical perspective, housing war relics, including a *Zero Fighter* plane, *Hien Fighter* plane, *Suisei* dive-bomber plane, an *Ohka* suicide rocket bomber, *Kaiten* suicide torpedo and many other items. The navy built *Ohka* and *Kaiten* for the sole purpose of the suicide mission.

Relics of the World War II & Kamikaze Missions

[160]The Mitsubishi A6M *Zero Fighter* was a light-weight, carrier-based fighter aircraft employed by the Imperial Japanese Navy Air Service from 1940 -1945. It was universally known as Zero from its Japanese Navy designation, Type Zero Carrier

---

159   John Breen. The dead and the living in the land of peace: a sociology of the Yasykuni shrine. Mortality, 2004, pp. 76-93

160   Wikipedia: A6M Zero. Online at http://en.wikipedia.org/wiki/Mitsubishi_Zero

Fighter, taken from the last digit of the Japan's Imperial year 2600 (1940), which is when it entered service. In Japan it was unofficially referred to as both *Rei-sen* and *Zero-sen*. Japanese students often used the expression "flying *Zero-sen*" for getting zero points or failing an exam. A combination of excellent manoeuvrability and very long range made it one of the finest fighters of its era. In early combat operations, the Zero gained a legendary reputation, outclassing its contemporaries.

Later, design weaknesses and the increasing scarcity of more powerful aircraft engines meant that the Zero became less effective against newer fighters. Later models of *Zero Fighter* were designed strictly for Kamikaze missions and many young men, including teenagers, boarded them to purposely crash into US aircraft carriers.

[161]The Kawasaki Ki-61 *Hien* "Swallow" fighter (named "Tony" by Allied Force) was employed by the Imperial Japanese Army Air Service from 1943 - 1945. The *Hien* entered combat in the spring of 1943 in the New Guinea war zone, covering New Guinea, the Admiralty Islands, New Britain, and New Ireland. The new Japanese fighter caused anxiety among Allied pilots, particularly when they found out that they could no longer go into a dive and escape as they had from lighter Japanese fighters. Although the *Hien* proved initially successful in combat against American fighters, it became increasingly outclassed.

When American pilots tested *Hien* after the war, however, they found out *Hien* was in fact an excellent fighter even in by post-war standards. They came to the conclusion that *Hien*'s poor performance at the end of the war was due to the fact that experienced Japanese pilots were in increasingly short supply. The empire had to pay the due for the Shinto *Jihad*, sending hundreds of good pilots into Kamikaze missions.

[162]Yokosuka D4Y1 Model 11 *Suisei* "Comet" carrier-based dive-bomber (named "Judy" by Allied Force) for the Imperial Japanese Navy Air Service became available in late 1942.

---

161   Greg Goebel / In The Public Domain. Online at http://www.vectorsite.net/index.html
162   Wikipedia: Yokosuka D4Y. Online at http://en.wikipedia.org/wiki/Mitsubishi_Zero

The first *Suisei* prototype made its maiden flight in December 1940, and proved to possess an excellent combination of high performance and good handling. The *Suisei* series of dive-bombers were very fast for this type of aircraft and some were even converted to night fighters against the American heavy-bombers later in the war.

Lacking armour and self-sealing fuel tanks, the *Suisei* did not do well against Allied fighter aircraft. They did, however, cause considerable damage to ships, including the carrier *USS Franklin*, which was nearly sunk by a single "Judy." The last version in the production was the D4Y4 Special Strike Bomber Model 43; a one-seat Kamikaze airplane capable of carrying a one 800-kg bomb. It was launched into production in February 1945. This magnificent Kamikaze plane was equipped with three rocket boosters for taking off from short runways and with terminal dive acceleration.

[163]*Ohka* was a small, rocket-powered vehicle mounting a large warhead in the nose and was intended to be carried to the target area by a larger plane. After being released, the *Ohka* would engage its rocket motors to make a high-speed dash to the target ship. The *Ohka* pilots, members of the *Jinrai Butai* or Thunder Gods Corps, are honored in Japan at Ohka Park in Kashima City, the Ohka Monument in Kanoya City, the Kamakura Ohka Monument at *Kencho-ji* Zen temple in Kamakura, and the Yasukuni Shrine in Tokyo. Many Japanese did not take the view that these *Ohka* pilots were brainwashed or that youths were fanatical zealots who had been coerced into action, but rather were heroic and selfless in the face of overwhelming odds. Others go further, such as [164]Yoshinori Kobayashi (born in 1953), one of Japan's most famous *manga* or comic artists, who presented in his comic books the *Ohka* and other Kamikazes as epitomizing the values that had been lost in modern Japan. They believed that the reason for their sacrifice was the self-defense of their country and loved ones by which he drew the line

---

163   Wikipedia: Ohka. Online at http://en.wikipedia.org/wiki/Ohka
164   Wikipedia: Yoshinori Kobayashi. Online at http://en.wikipedia.org/wiki/Yoshinori_ Kobayashi

from Islamic radical fundamentalists who employed the same method. They did not specifically take or copy their attitude from Islamic fundamentalists. However, there were many dangerous similarities between Kamikazes and radical Islam and both appear to have been brainwashed by their superiors and forced to abandon autonomy and their own rational minds.

[165] *Kaiten* type human torpedoes were the first Japanese Special Attack weapons, vehicles whose operational use involved the certain death of the crew, though their first successful employment followed that of the Kamikaze suicide aircraft by about a month. Proposals for human torpedoes were made in 1943 and were approved in early 1944, initially with provision for the survival of the operator. However, the extremely desperate situation of Japan after the loss of the *Marianas* in June 1944 led to acceptance of the pilot's death as an inevitable consequence of *Kaiten* use.

[166] Yokosuka D4Y1 Model 11 Suisei. Yasukuni Jinja Yushukan Zuroku, 2008.[167]

---

165   Wikipedia: Kaiten. http://search.yahoo.com/search;_ylt=AucDkV6Zn7mRD_8q1 tMz9VabvZx4?fp_ip=ca&p=kaiten&toggle=1&cop=mss&ei=UTF-8&fr=yfp-t-701
166   Was available June 2010: http://www.kirei-ni.com/portrait/shouzouga/Gy-12sa/ GY12-2.jpg
167   The picture is used under "fair dealing" (Canada) and "fair use" (USA) provisions in copyright law.

Yusukuni as the Center of Shinto *Jihad*

The Yushukan honoured all of Japan's war dead as heroes who died for a good cause. There was also one display case in the museum that dealt exclusively with the special attack corps well known as [168]*Kamikaze Party*, which carried out suicide attacks in World War II. Six exhibition galleries and the Great Exhibition Hall contained displays of some photos, letters, or other items related to the special attack forces. Also, the 3,000 or so small photos displayed in three exhibition galleries at the museum included war dead from both the Imperial Japanese Navy and Army. Each photo gave the person's name, military branch (Navy or Army), rank, date and place of death, and home prefecture. [169]Herbert Bix noted that:

> Kamikaze attacks on Allied warships and troop transporters were an entirely different threat, however a real and dangerous one. They were a kind of weapon American, Australians and Britons simply could not understand, and for that reason found all the more disturbing (Bix, 2000).

Interestingly, Kamikaze Party used similar methods as al-Qaeda that attacked the World Trade Centre and Pentagon in 2001. The Islamic terrorist organization had copied 60 year-old Japanese suicide missions and crashed hijacked planes into two American targets. Kamikaze pilots who crashed their planes into American aircraft carriers indeed performed a type of Shinto *Jihad*, their own holy mission. The formation of special attack corps with suicide missions indicated that Japan's Shinto State was a cult with similar nature and social and psychological characteristics as the terrorist organization led by [170]Osama bin Laden, although the Shinto belief system was quite different from Islam. Cult organizations demanded their followers' blind submission and asked them to sacrifice anything including their lives for their cause, telling them they would be greatly rewarded in the afterlife.

---

168   *Kamikaze*: 神風 meant "wind of Kami or god."
169   Herbert P. Bix Hirohito and the Making of Modern Japan p. 482
170   Wikipedia: Osama bin Laden. Online at June 2007: http://en.wikipedia.org/wiki/Osama_bin_Laden

[171]In summary, the Yushukan presented a highly slanted and twisted view of Japan's military history, with highlights of heroic moments, justified aggressions on China and surrounding regions of East Asia, a romanticised Kamikaze Party, represented as true heroes who died for the country and the great cause, but no mention of negative incidents such as foreign comfort women or sex partners for Japanese soldiers abducted from various Asian countries and Australia during the Second World War and [172]Unit 731[173] in Manchuria. [174]The museum gave Howard French, a New York Times reporter the impression that "Japan sacrificed its blood and treasures throughout the 20th century not to conquer other Asian countries but to fight for their independence."

Yushukan also had a theatre that displayed a nationalist perspective of Japan's war history and tried to portray a military history of which Japanese people should be proud. The theatre has continuous showings of a 50-minute film entitled "We Shall Not Forget," which gives the Japanese nationalist perspective that Japan was not at fault in the Nanking massacre in 1937 and that Japanese leaders were wrongly convicted at the Tokyo war crimes trials. The museum has an exhibit that portrays Japan as the key to the liberation of other Asian countries from the U.S. and European powers.

---

171   Bill Gordon. Kamikaze Images Online at http://wgordon.web.wesleyan.edu/kamikaze/museums/yushukan/index.htm
172   Unit 731 was a covert medical experiment unit of the Imperial Japanese Army led by Lieutenant General Shiro Ishii (1892-1959). The unit researched biological warfare through human experimentation during the Second Sino-Japanese War (1937-1945) and World War II. Ishii who committed one of most horrendous crimes in human history did not receive any sentence. It was believed that because the data Ishii's obtained through human experimentation was valuable for the US military, he earned immunity from war-crimes prosecution after a secret negotiation took place. Ishii died peacefully in Tokyo in 1959.
173   Wikipedia: Unit 731. Online at http://en.wikipedia.org/wiki/Unit_731
174   Howard French. At a Military Museum, the Losers Write History. Tokyo Journal: New York Times (Oct 30, 2002)

[175] Yokosuka MXY-7 Ohka. [176]

Yasukuni as the Centre of Conflicts

When Prime Minister Koizumi first made an official visit to Yasukuni Shrine in 2001, there were both domestic and International protests against his visit. Japanese Ambassadors in China and South Korea were summoned to ministries of foreign affairs to hear official protests. Also in 2001, on the streets of Seoul, protesters gathered to denounce the Prime Minister's visit to the shrine. Japanese flags were burned in the streets, and 20 young men cut off their finger tips and mailed them to the Japanese Embassy in protest. In Beijing, students gathered in front of the Japanese Embassy and burned a Japanese flag.

In December 2005, during the East Asian Summit, President Roh Moo Hyun of South Korea and Chinese Prime

---

175   Was available June 2010; http://img02.hamazo.tv/usr/
        kanzin/%E6%A1%9C%E8%8A%B1.jpg
176   The picture is used under "fair dealing" (Canada) and "fair use" (USA)
        provisions in copyright law.

Minister Wen Jiabao refused an official meeting with Koizumi. But Koizumi adamantly insisted on visiting the Yasukuni Shrine despite these international resistances. He refused to recognize that the protests in the streets and among Foreign Ministries demonstrated a clear and present danger to the international relations between Japan and its neighbours. In spring of 2006, Foreign Minister Aso Taro suggested that Emperor Akihito should visit Yasukuni. [177]William Daniel Sturgeon (2006) remarked that Koizumi straddled and muddled the international and domestic paradoxes of the Yasukuni problem.

As [178]Sturgeon noted, Yasukuni had been the centre of conflicts and feuds for decades and an extremely stormy place after World War II. It would not be an overstatement that the history of Yasukuni after the war was the centre of both domestic and international disputes, particularly after 1985 when Prime Minister Nakasone made his first official visit there. Sturgeon remarked that Japan's past prime ministers and other government officials who visited the shrine demonstrated a questionable lack of repentance for the war. By visiting the shrine, especially in an official capacity, they demonstrated an acceptance of the rightist view articulated in Yasukuni's *Yushukan War Memorabilia Museum*, which justified Japan's aggression to the East Asia during World War II. Sturgeon viewed that by visiting Yasukuni, Koizumi was endorsing and promoting a point of view that rejected Japan's responsibility for the war against China and the Pacific War. In her unpublished doctoral dissertation, [179]Jennifer Lind wrote:

> A state's failure to atone for past violence
> provokes hatred, anger, and wounded pride
> among its former victims. These emotions distort
> the process of threat assessment. Fear and
> antipathy lead countries to infer malign intentions
> from ambiguous behavior" (Lind, 2003).

177   William Daniel Sturgeon. Japan's Yasukuni Shrine: Place of Peace or Place of Conflict? (Dissertations.com, 2006) p. 90
178   Sturgeon, Japan's Yasukuni Shrine. pp. 87-90
179   Jennifer Lind. Sorry States: Apologies in International Politics. Unpublished doctoral dissertation, Massachusetts Institute of Technology, 2003

Summarizing her statement, the lack of remorse about past actions among today's leaders, gives Japan's neighbors reason to pause and consider the intention of Japanese leaders, although the nation now has a peace constitution and has not fought any war for over 60 years.

[180] Mitsubishi A6M Zero Fighter.

Yasukuni Jinja Yushukan Zuroku, 2008.[181]

---

180   Was available June 2010: http://www.kirei-ni.com/portrait/shouzouga/Gy-12sa/
      GY12-2.jpg
181   The picture is used under "fair dealing" (Canada) and "fair use" (USA)
      provisions in copyright law.

CHAPTER 6

ENSHRINEMENT OF CLASS-A WAR CRIMINALS

Yasukuni Shrine has been the centre of controversies mainly because 14 convicted [182]Class-A war criminals ("crimes against peace") were enshrined there as gods along with the practice of Emperor Worship in the past. But for the majority who oppose the official visit of a prime minister, Emperor Worship was a relic of the past. Although the emperor system continues to exist today as a symbol of the state, most Yasukuni critics either in Japan or her neighbours do not feel immediate danger. The enshrinement of 14 convicted Class-A war criminals, however, almost instantaneously provoked anger among those who still remember the ugliness of the Pacific War started by Japanese leaders enshrined as *Kami*. For many survivors of the war, these 14 people were equal to the devil who destroyed their life by slaughtering their family, friends and all their loved ones. Their enshrinement looked like a form of demon worship or as bad as the [183]*Satanism Cult*.

Martyrs of Showa

[184]On October 17, 1978, 14 accused of Class A war crimes (according to the judgment of the International Military Tribunal for the Far East), including Hideki Tojo and Kiichiro Hiranuma, were quietly enshrined as *Showa Junnansha* "Martyrs of Showa", ostensibly on the technicality that they were on the registry. They are listed below, according to their sentences:

---

182   A crime against peace, in international law, referred to the act of military invasion as a war crime, specifically referring to starting or waging war against the integrity, independence, or sovereignty of a territory or state, or else a military violation of relevant international treaties, agreements or legally binding assurances.

183   Wikipedia: Satanism. Online at http://en.wikipedia.org/wiki/Satanist

184   Wikipedia: Yasukuni Shrine. Online at http://en.wikipedia.org/wiki/Yasukuni_Shrine

Death by hanging:
   Hideki Tojo, Seishiro Itagaki, Heitaro Kimura, Kenji
   Doihara, Iwane Matsui, Akira Muto, Koki Hirota

Lifetime imprisonment:
   Yoshijiro Umezu, Kuniaki Koiso, Kiichiro
   Hiranuma, Toshio Shiratori

20-year imprisonment:
   Shigenori Togo

Died before a judicial decision was reached
(due to illness or disease):
   Osami Nagano, Yosuke Matsuoka

This was revealed to the media on April 19, 1979, and a controversy started in 1983 when Prime Minister Nakasone made an official visit. The shrine officials kept on defending their enshrinements, insisting that the even Hiranuma and Tojo were "martyrs" who gave up their lives for the good cause to liberate Japan and her neighbours from the evil force of the USA and Europe. As [185]Frank Baldwin (1986) noted, the shrine officials had no regret about their action of treating 14 criminals as *Kami* or gods - giving them a special place.

The Shrine insisted that those 14 accused of Class-A war crimes were not evildoers who committed crimes against humanity, but "martyrs" with a noble cause who were cruelly and wrongfully tried as war criminals. For the general public in both Japan and her neighbours, Yasukuni's intention to defend these 14 people, honour them and insist on their innocence seemed completely ridiculous and outrageous. It seemed almost beyond the comprehension of almost anyone except those who believed in pre-Second World War State Shinto or ultra-nationalist Emperor Cult. Some of them like Kiichiro Hiranuma had indeed exhibited an evil character along with their crimes. He forced the

---

185   Baldwin. State and Religion in Japan: A Crack in the Wall?"

Japanese public to accept the State Shinto or emperor centered evil cult, and persecuted followers of Christ and all others who opposed the cult.

Bios of Convicted Criminals against Peace & Humanity

[186]General Hideki Tojo (東條英機) (1884–1948) became the prime minister of Japan shortly before the beginning of the Pacific War. Unlike Hiranuma, one of his predecessors, Tojo did not possess an evil character or religious fanaticism. But his deed was evil enough for the death penalty, for he led Japan into total disaster by the commencement of the war against the United States and other nations in the Allied Forces. In public, he was propagating the message that there was no solution other than the war when Japan was facing a series of still unsolvable disputes with the United States. Tojo also used his special police called [187]Kempeitai (憲兵隊) to jail all his political opponents or [188]sent them to battlefields as lowest rank soldiers and let them die. It was safe to conclude that if a Japanese prosecutor and judges tried two of them in Japanese court, they would have similar verdicts as well, because there was absolutely no evidence to validate their innocence. They were convicted because they committed crimes against peace and humanity.

[189]In October 1941, Emperor Hirohito appointed Tojo as the prime minister of Japan when Japan and the United States had a serious diplomatic conflict when Japan's military aggressions continued in Manchuria and Indo-China. When he was appointed as the leader, both Japan and the United States pursued to establish military and economic [190]hegemony or dominance over China, which was weakened by the series of internal conflicts and civil wars after the eighteenth century. Leaders from both sides tried to reach an agreement for peace in the Pacific Region and China so that they could avoid the war. But they failed to reach

186   Wikipedia: Hideki Tojo. Online at http://en.wikipedia.org/wiki/Hideki_Tojo
187   Wikipedia: Kempeitai. Online at http://en.wikipedia.org/wiki/Kempeitai
188   Tojo's action was as evil as King David who sent Uriah to a battlefield and let him die therein Second Samuel 11.
189   Ikuhiko Hata. Gendaishi no soten [Controversies of Today's History]. (Tokyo: Bungeshunju, 2001) pp. 238-253
190   Wikipedia: Hegemony. Online at http://en.wikipedia.org/wiki/Hegemony

to do so because both sides intended not to loose the ground of hegemony over China and imperialistic expenditure.

Tojo's appointment was the idea that belonged to [191]Koichi Kido (1889 – 1977), the *Lord Keeper of the Privy Seal* of Japan who administrated the whole palace. It was generally believed that Kido conceived his appointment was the only way not to start the war because Tojo had great power within the army.

[192]Peter Wetzer (1998) noted that Tojo built a reputation as a hardworking and very efficient army officer. He favoured technical innovation and modernization over emphasis on the unique spiritual qualities of the Japanese soldier. He was highly educated in modern technology of war and equally well indoctrinated in the ideology of Kokutai and the supposed superiority of the Japanese spirit called *Yamato-damashii*. In short, he possessed almost all the desired attributes or qualities of a typical elite army officer of Japan in the early 20th century.

Pacific war was on the verge of breaking out in 1941 as the army division of Japan's military aggressively pressed against Allied Forces. Tojo was one of the strong advocates of the war. But as well, he was known for an exceptional loyalty to the emperor. Kido believed that if the emperor did not want war, Tojo would not pursue it as prime minister. Hirohito agreed with Kido and appointed Tojo on the condition that he must give up the agenda to seek war[193].

After the appointment as prime minister, Tojo submitted to Hirohito's order and made a considerable effort to find alternative options other than starting a war. Hirohito also ordered Tojo not to declare the war even in the case that Washington demanded to draw Japan's whole forces from China. Tojo agreed. Hirohito asked Tojo for a justification of war against the Allied Forces. Tojo stated he was going to find the most plausible rationale for it.

---

191   Wikipedia: Koichi Kido. Online at http://en.wikipedia.org/wiki/Koichi_Kido
192   Peter Wetzler. Hirohito and War (Honolulu: University of Hawaii Press, 1998) p. 64
193   Herbert P. Bix Hirohito and the Making of Modern Japan (NY: HarperCollins Publishers, 2000)

[194]According to popular belief in Japan, Kido viewed Tojo as the most loyal person to the emperor among all Japan's Army generals of his day. Colonel Sadao Akamatsu (1949-1982), who was once Tojo's secretary, referred to several virtuous characteristics of Tojo. He was with a strong sense of responsibility, not greedy, studious, sympathetic, action oriented, ready for any circumstance and finally, loyal to the emperor. General Isamu Taniguchi, however, whose father was a best friend of Tojo's father, was well versed in his weaknesses as well as his strengths. Taniguchi observed that Tojo's greatest weakness was a narrow-mindedness and inability to control emotions in certain circumstances. He viewed Tojo an overly passionate, zealous and opinionated individual who easily allowed his personal feelings and opinions to prevent him from seeing things clearly and making objective judgments.

It was also generally believed that Kido strongly recommended Tojo's appointment to Hirohito because he believed in his good character. However, some suggested the possibility that one of Tojo's subordinates secretly visited and threatened Kido by implying a coup if Tojo was not appointed as prime minister. It was also believed that Japan's military, particularly its army division, controlled the whole country. Some others suggested that Kido recommended Tojo because he believed in the commencement of the war and therefore Japan's defeat, as the consequence of the appointment was inevitable. Kido did it to make Tojo responsible and punishable for the eventual war crimes.

There was an almost endless debate as to whether or not Hirohito was a real pacifist who was totally against the war with no interest at all in the expansion of the empire. The view by [195]Herbert Bix (2001) is that Hirohito's image was as a pacifist - a helpless figurehead who did nothing about the war, was the myth Japan's post-war establishment created. I myself strongly agree with Bix that Hirohito was not an innocent or "saintly"

---

194   Ikuhiko Hata. Gendaishi no soten [Controversies of Today's History]
       pp. 238-253
195   Herbert P. Bix Hirohito and the Making of Modern Japan

person. It is safe to believe, however, that Hirohito had a more practical perspective on the war than military leaders advocate. He did not believe that Japan would win if the war started. He was well aware of the USA's military might in comparison with Japan. Should the war break out, there was little likelihood that Japan would win. Therefore, he was not likely to have agreed with the war until he was finally persuaded by some of war advocates in late 1941 and became convinced that Japan could win. He was persuaded almost in a similar way that a rationally minded person with good common sense, healthy skepticism and critical thinking is finally induced to join pyramid or multiple level marketing scheme by an enthusiastic and charismatic sales person.

Tojo once seriously considered obedience to Hirohito's order to avert the war by any means, but failed to persuade his colleagues who already had their minds set up to start the war against the Allied Forces. Negotiation between Japan's foreign affairs department and the US broke up. [196]At the beginning of November 1941, Tojo and his associates came to the conclusion that war was inevitable. Tojo reported this to the emperor who initially protested but ultimately sanctioned the decision.

Tojo went to war against the US and Britain, apparently not following Hirohito's order. Contrary to the concern of Hirohito and other skeptics, when war was declared, Japan fought quite well for about six months until she suffered a severe loss in the battle of Midway. Hirohito was very happy with the initial successions of victories and commended Tojo for his success. He remarked that his country was winning in a very difficult war because Tojo was such a good leader. [197]Ikuhiko Hata (秦郁彦) (2001) contends that Japan's winning at the beginning of the war was the "honeymoon" between Tojo and Hirohito. But the "honeymoon" came to an end as soon as Japan started losing the battles.

---

196   Peter Wetzler.Hirohito and War (Honolulu:University of Hawaii Press,1998)
       p. 56
197   Ikuhiko Hata. Gendaishi no soten [Controversies of Today's History]
       pp. 238-253

[198]Bix states that Hirohito's mind was already fixed on war in early November 1941. On November 8 he received detailed information about the Pearl Harbor attack plan and responded that the plan was extremely bold and impressive as was the Battle of Okehazama in which [199]Oda Nobunaga (織田信長) (1534–1582), a medieval warlord who eventually became the ruler of Japan, won over Imagawa Yoshimoto with much greater force. Hirohito's loyalists in Japan might defend him by saying that his statement was sarcasm or an indirect expression of disapproval of the plan. It is difficult to understand the true intention of the emperor, and therefore he remained an enigmatic individual all his life. But it would be a fair judgment to say that Hirohito was at least guilty of approving the irrational war at the end even though he did not actively promote it.

It could be said that Hirohito had a political, moral and legal responsibility regarding sanctioning the war in a similar way that on December 7, 2005, [200]Hidetsugu Ageha, a Japanese first-class architect and builder, was accused of falsifying structural data regarding the earthquake resistance of various condominiums and hotels. Many Japanese were sympathetic to Ageha because it seemed evident that he was intimidated by his contractors to do so. But he was still guilty of the crime of falsifying the structural data and putting many buildings in danger.

Also, Hata's study parallels with [201]Herbert Bix's view. It would be safe to view him at least responsible for the appointment of Tojo, no matter what kind of intention he had. [202]On his decision to appoint Tojo as the prime minister, Hirohito quoted an ancient [203]Chinese Proverb "If you don't go into the cave of the tiger, how are you going to get its cub?" Hirohito viewed Tojo as a "tiger cub" who was competent, diligent, and

---

198   Herbert P. Bix Hirohito and the Making of Modern Japan
199   Wikipedia: Oda Nobunaga. Online at http://en.wikipedia.org/wiki/Oda_
       Nobunaga
200   Wikipedia: Hidetsugu Aneha. Online at http://en.wikipedia.org/wiki/Hidetsugu_
       Aneha
201   Herbert P. Bix Hirohito and the Making of Modern Japan.
202   Ikuhiko Hata. Gendaishi no soten [Controversies of Today's History]
       pp. 238-253
203   Simran Khurana. Top 10 Chinese Proverbs. Online at http://quotations.about.
       com/cs/chineseproverbs/tp/10_chinese.htm

sincere as well as the most loyal person to the emperor among all Japan's Army generals in those days.

Hirohito did, however, view the Army as the same type of dangerous and destructive entity as a "tiger's cave," with a possibility to ruin the entire country. According to this metaphor, he chose to go to the cave and took a cub, and tigers destroyed the entire nation. Any person who owns a tiger or any other exotic cat as a pet must be responsible for the pet's actions. The owner cannot be exonerated from his responsibility by saying, "It's not me, but my tiger ate a person".

Tojo was not democratically elected leader because Japan did not have a democratic constitution at that time. Under the Meiji constitution the imperial diet existed, but did not have the power to elect the prime minister. The power to select the prime minister belonged to a group appointed by the emperor. There was no democratic procedure to elect the prime minister until 1945 when the new constitution was introduced. Tojo lacked the ability to obtain public approvals because he had never been elected to any government office. In addition, his military career was longer than politics, and he was still an active Army officer while he was the prime minister. When Japan started losing in the war, critics fiercely attacked him.

Tojo did not have a long enough political experience to fight a political battle, though he had a long experience of fighting military battles. For him, the only way to survive in the political world was the use of *Kenpeitai* or the military's special police. His only chance of survival was the use of military tactics in politics due to his lack of his political skills.

[204]As Japan's military lost more battles, Tojo's position became more difficult. His popularity declined so that he lost the confidence and support from the emperor at the end. Between the defeats in the Solomon Islands early in 1943 and the fall of Saipan in July 1944, a small group of court officials and senior statesmen led by former prime minister [205]Prince Fumimaro

---

204   Herbert P. Bix Hirohito and the Making of Modern Japan p. 478
205   Wikipedia: Fumimaro Konoe. Online at http://en.wikipedia.org/wiki/Fumimaro_
      Konoe

Konoe (近衞文麿) (1891–1945) and a group of navy officers including former prime minister [206]Admiral Keisuke Okada (岡田啓介) (1868–1952), worked covertly to expel Tojo from his office. They told the emperor that unless Tojo was dismissed, Japan would lose the entire war. According to Bix, these men knew that Tojo's power flowed from the support of the far greater power of the emperor, so that Hirohito had the power to dismiss the prime minister. Disappointed with the state of the war, Hirohito finally withdrew his support of Tojo and allowed his government to collapse on July 18, 1944 nearly a year before Japan's final defeat in August 1945.

[207]Tojo had created his own spy agency to watch over his opponents and critics. Masataka Nakano was a popular diet member who complimented Tojo in the Asahi News Paper as a great wartime prime minister. But Tojo took Nakano's compliment as sarcasm, ordered *Kenpeitai* to arrest him and banned his books. Prosecutors investigated Nakano's guilt under Japan's law during the war, but could not find any evidence to prosecute him. Nakano committed *harakiri* in front of *Kenpeitai* guards. Toneo Nakamura, one of prosecutors who failed in a job in prosecuting Nakano was conscripted as a soldier with lowest rank in the army and sent to a battlefield. Likewise, Dr. Shigeyoshi Matsumae (松前重義) (1901-1991) one of Nation's well known engineers and important government employees for the development of new and efficient weaponry systems, was conscripted and sent to the battle field in the same way as Nakamura, because the authority discovered Matsumae was a member of one of anti-Tojo groups. However, Matsumae survived, became one of Socialist party's diet members, founder of International Judo Association and Tokai University after the war.

[208]Hata raises some question if the series of evil deeds

---

206   Wikipedia: Keisuke Okada. Online at http://en.wikipedia.org/wiki/Okada_
       Keisuke
207   Ikuhiko Hata. Gendaishi no soten [Controversies of Today's History]
       pp. 238-253
208   Ikuhiko Hata. Gendaishi no soten [Controversies of Today's History]
       pp. 238-253

were planned by Tojo himself or some of his subordinates in the background. He maintained that Tojo lacked discernment in selecting his own subordinates. Therefore, eccentric, egocentric and inadequate people surrounded him. However, Hata concludes sending Nakamura, Matsumae and others to battle was an action that fit perfectly with Toji's personality that could not tolerate oppositions and disagreements and knew nothing about democracy.

According to [209]Hirohito Monologue by Hidenari Terasaki (寺崎英成) (1900-1951), a liaison officer of the imperial household, Hirohito was rather sympathetic to Tojo. He commented that Tojo was a rational and reasonable person who listened well and understood logic. Hirohito analyzed Tojo's downfall as threefold: Japan's loss of the Marian Islands; the overuse of *Kempeitai* or military police and [210]wearing too many hats that disallowed him to communicate with citizens directly. Also the Emperor believed Tojo's subordinates rather than Tojo himself were responsible for the series of scandals, including the conscriptions of his opponents.

It must be noted that Kiyoshi Inoue (井上清) (1913-2001), Japan's well known and respected Marxist historian, was very harsh to Hirohito and more sympathetic to Tojo than Hata and other pro-Hirohito historians. [211]Inoue maintains that it was completely impossible for Tojo to go to war totally ignoring Hirohito's decision. Tojo, according to Inoue, was very desirous to follow the emperor's will and asked Hirohito's approval in every decision he made. Therefore, Inoue views that Tojo was made a villain by GHQ (General Headquarter of the Occupation Force) to save Hirohito from criminal charges.

Another convicted Class-A War Criminal who was tried by the International Military Tribunal for the Far East was [212] General

209   Hidenari Terasaki & Mariko Terasaki Miller, eds., Showa Tenno Dokuhakuroku [Monologue of Showa Emperor]. (Tokyo: Bunshun Bunko, 1995) pp. 102-105
210   While being Prime Minister, Tojo was also Army Minister and Internal Affair Minister at the same time.
211   Kiyoshi Inoue. Tenno no sensosekinin [Emperor's responsibility for the War] (Tokyo: Iwanami Bunko, 2004) pp. 266-267
212   Wikepedia: Itagaki Seishiro. Online at http://en.wikipedia.org/wiki/Itagaki_Seishiro

Seishiro Itagaki (板垣征四郎) (1885-1948), a Japanese military officer in the Guandong Army who became an active advocate of aggressive action against China. He was appointed minister of war in 1938 and then chief of staff of the China Expeditionary Army in 1939. Itagaki was named Commander-in-Chief of the 17th Area Army in Korea in 1945 and Commander-in-Chief of 7th Area Army in Singapore later that same year. He was charged with having waged wars against China, the USSR, France, the British Commonwealth and the Netherlands by the *International Military Tribunal for the Far East*. He was condemned to death and hanged as a war criminal in 1948. Itagaki was also responsible for the negligence of supply of food and medical care to prisoners of war and civilian internees, in particular on various Indonesian islands during the last months of the war.

[213]General Heitaro Kimura (木村兵太郎) (1888-1948) was a Japanese Army Officer who was made chief of staff of the *Kwantung Army* in 1940. He assisted in the planning of the war against China and the Pacific War as Vice-Minister of War from 1941 to 1943. From 1943 to 1944 he was a member of the Supreme War Council. He became the commander-in-chief of the Burma Area Army in 1944. He was responsible for the construction of the *Death Railway*, which led to the death and brutalization of thousands of prisoners of war. He attained the rank of general in 1945. In 1948, he was condemned to death by the International Military Tribunal for the Far East and hanged as a war criminal.

[214]General Kenji Doihara (土肥原賢二) (1883 -1948) was a Japanese Army officer and spy who served in northeastern China from 1913 and who became a major military commander in Japan's invasion of China over the following decades. He was one of the main plotters of the so-called *Mukden Incident*, the pretext for the Japanese invasion of Manchuria prior to the Second World War. Doihara was nicknamed *Lawrence of Manchuria*, with a reference to Lieutenant-Colonel [215]Thomas

---

213   Wikepedia: Heitaro Kimura. Online at http://en.wikipedia.org/wiki/Heitaro_
       Kimura
214   Wikepedia: Kenji Doihara. Online at http://en.wikipedia.org/wiki/Kenji_Doihara
215   Wikepedia: T. E. Lawrence. Online at http://en.wikipedia.org/wiki/Kenji_Doihara

Edward Lawrence (1888 – 1935), the British soldier known as *Lawrence of Arabia*.

[216]General Iwane Matsui (松井石根) (1878-1948) was an Army officer of the Japanese Imperial Army and the commander of the expeditionary forces sent to China. He was sentenced to death by hanging by the *International Military Tribunal for the Far East* for being responsible for the *Nanking Massacre*. On August 23, 1937, Japan's *Shanghai Expeditionary Force* (SEF) was sent to Shanghai. Then, on November 7 of the same year, the *Central China Area Army* (CCAA) was organized by combining the SEF and the 10th Army, with Matsui appointed as its commander-in-chief concurrently with that of the SEF. While Matsui himself was not present during the beginning of the atrocities as he was ill at the time, he was aware of what his men were doing in the city, as were members of the Japanese Foreign Service who had followed the army into the city. Word began to trickle out of Nanking, and growing pressure was placed on the Imperial government to recall the SEF officers.

Concerning atrocities in Nanking, Matsui noted in his war journal, with great regret, about the rapes and looting that took place and therefore destroyed the reputation of the Imperial Army. He also mentioned "a number of abominable incidents within the past 50 days" at the memorial service for the war-dead of the SEF held on February 7, 1937 and in tears charged the officers and the soldiers, saying that the atrocities done by some of the soldiers had brought down the reputation of the empire. He said such things should not happen in the Imperial Army - they should keep the disciplines strictly and should never persecute innocent people.

[217]General Akira Muto (武藤章) (1883 –1948) was a Japanese army commander. He joined the Japanese Army and in 1913 joined the *General High Staff*. He also served under Fumimaro Konoe as head of the *Military Affairs Bureau*. Muto worked as a military adviser to Hideki Tojo, serving as the Philippines Expeditionary Force's leader. After the Second World War, Muto was arrested and charged with crimes against peace.

216   Wikepedia: Iwane Matsui. Online at http://en.wikipedia.org/wiki/Matsui_Iwane
217   Wikepedia: Akira Muto. Online at http://en.wikipedia.org/wiki/Akira_Muto

He was convicted and executed by hanging on December 23, 1948.

[218]Kōki Hirota (広田弘毅) (1878–1948) was a Japanese politician and the prime minister of Japan from March 9, 1936 to February 2, 1937. Unlike most other convicted Class-A Criminals who were given a death sentence, he was a civilian rather than a military officer. He entered the Ministry of Foreign Affairs to become a career diplomat, and served as ambassador to the Soviet Union from 1928 to 1932 before becoming foreign minister in 1933, the same year of Japan's withdrawal from the League of Nations.

In 1936, following the February 26 Incident, the emperor Hirohito named Hirota as prime minister. Hirota's government, with the blessing of the emperor, signed its first treaty with Germany. Hirota's second tenure as foreign minister would eventually lead to his death. Like Matsui, though he was not in charge of the army units that invaded Nanjing at the time of the *Nanking Massacre*, he was a part of responsible chain of command, and informed the Japanese embassy in Washington of the extensive carnage in the city. Following Japan's surrender, Hirota was named a Class-A war criminal and was brought before the *International Military Tribunal for the Far East*. He was found guilty and executed by hanging at Sugamo Prison.

[219]General Yoshijiro Umezu (梅津美治郎) (1882-1949) was the chief commander of the Japanese army in the Second World War. Umezu opposed surrender in August of 1945; he believed that the military should fight on, forcing the Allies to sustain heavy losses in a ground invasion of Japan, and that only this way could Japan negotiate for better peace terms. After the war he was tried as a war criminal along with other senior Japanese officials and sentenced to life imprisonment on November 12, 1948. He died from an illness in 1949.

---

218   Wikepedia: Koki Hirota. Online at http://en.wikipedia.org/wiki/Koki_Hirota
219   Wikepedia: Yoshijiro Umezu. Online at http://en.wikipedia.org/wiki/Yoshijiro_ Umezu

[220]General Kuniaki Koiso (小磯國昭) (1880–1950) was an Army officer in the Imperial Japanese Army, Governor-General of Korea and Prime Minister of Japan from July 22, 1944 to April 7, 1945. In February 1932, Koiso became Vice-Minister of War and in August 1932, concurrently Chief of Staff of the Kwantung Army. In March 1934, he was transferred to command the 5th Division in Hiroshima. He then assumed command of the *Chosen Army* in December 1935. Promoted to full general in November 1937, he joined the Army General Staff in July 1938. Koiso left active duty in July 1938. From April to August 1939, he served as minister of the newly created cabinet post of Ministry of Greater East Asia, and again from January to July 1940.

Koiso was Governor-General of Korea from May 1942 to1944. In July 1944, he was chosen to serve as Prime Minister of Japan after the downfall of the Tojo cabinet. The civilian cabinet ministers, especially Koichi Kido and former prime minister Fumimaro Konoe did not favour Koiso, due to Koiso's previous involvement with the *Sakura Kai* and its attempted coup d'état against the government in 1931. Emperor Hirohito shared these reservations in his Privy Council meetings. Nevertheless, Koiso was selected, as no consensus could be reached on a more suitable alternative.

According to [221]Hirohito Monologue by Terasaki, Hirohito was not at all in favour of Koiso because of his Shinto based occult or psychic spiritualism and lack of understanding on economics. Hirohito also commented that Koiso listened to him, but did not possess his own opinion and totally lacked confidence and courage. The emperor was also aware of Koiso's alleged involvement in right wing or "ultra-ultra-nationalist" terrorism which intended to replace Hirohito with more authoritarian and the spiritualist emperor of the past. Hirohito viewed Koiso as a despicable "little pitiful thing" or completely unsuitable person for the position of national leadership.

220   Wikepedia: Kuniaki Koiso. Online at http://en.wikipedia.org/wiki/Koiso_Kuniaki
221   Hidenari Terasaki & Mariko Terasaki Miller, eds., Showa Tenno Dokuhakuroku [Monologue of Showa Emperor]. (Tokyo: Bunshun Bunko, 1995) pp. 114-117

During Koiso's term, Japanese forces faced multiple defeats on all fronts at the hands of both the United States army and navy. Koiso was an ardent supporter of State Shintoism along with Heisuke Yanagawa, who directed the Government Imperial Aid Association. He restored the ancient sacred rites in the Sukumo River, near Hakone, the "Preliminary Misogi Rite." As an ardent follower of State Shintoism, Koiso believed that Shinto sacred rites in a river could improve the nation's war circumstances. He also imposed State Shinto to the Koreans as Governor-General of Korea. In terms of imposing this cult and religious beliefs to the public, Koiso was as guilty as Hiranuma and worse than Tojo.

After the end the war, Koiso was arrested by the Supreme Commander of the Allied Powers and tried by the International Military Tribunal for war crimes. Upon conviction as a Class-A war criminal, he was given a sentence of life imprisonment. The Tribunal specifically cited Koiso's "brutality" during his period of rule over Korea, and the fact that, as Prime Minister, he was aware of the mistreatment of prisoners of war by the Japanese military. Koiso died in Sugamo Prison in 1950. Although I generally don't support the death penalty, I perceive it unfair that Hiranuma and Koiso, who seemed to have committed the most heinous crimes against the humanity, died in prison, while Tojo and six others were hanged.

[222]Toshio Shiratori (白鳥敏夫) (1887-1949) was the Japanese ambassador to Italy from 1938 to 1940, advisor to the Japanese foreign minister in 1940, and one of the 14 Class-A war criminals enshrined at Yasukuni in 1978. He served as *Director of Information Bureau* under the Foreign Ministry from 1929 to 1933. He was appointed ambassador to Italy, serving from 1938 to 1940, and became adviser to the foreign minister in 1940. He was an advocate of military expansionism, counselling an alliance between Nazi Germany, Italy and Japan to facilitate world domination. The International Military Tribunal found him guilty of war crimes. He was sentenced to imprisonment for life for

---

222   Wikepedia: Toshio Shiratori. Online at http://en.wikipedia.org/wiki/Toshio_
      Shiratori

waging wars of aggression, and wars in violation of international law. He died in prison. A memo from Emperor Hirohito, disclosed in 2006, revealed that he stopped visiting the Yasukuni Shrine because of the enrolment of the war criminals, stating "they even enshrined Matsuoka and Shiratori."

Shigenori Togo (東郷茂徳) (1882 -1950), who was the Minister of Foreign Affairs when the war broke out, could be viewed more sympathetically than any other convicted Class-A Criminals on a personal level because he had some noble intentions, although he was still responsible for his guilty actions. He was not an advocate of war against the United States. Throughout the war, Shigenori Togo was among those who doubted that Japan could succeed in a war with the United States. However, he agreed to sign the document of the declaration of war when Japan's negotiation with the United States failed and Prime Minister Tojo made a decision to send a fleet to attack Pearl Harbor. He was sentenced to 20 years and died of illness in prison.

According to [223]Bix, Togo was also guilty of intentionally misinterpreting "Hull notes" in the American ultimatum when it arrived on November 26, 1941. Hull handed Ambassador [224]Kichisaburo Nomura (野村吉三郎) (1877-1964) a "draft mutual declaration of policy" and a ten-point written outline of principles as a comprehensive agreement. The document was headed "strictly confidential, tentative and without commitment." It called for Japan to "withdraw all military, naval, air and police forces from China and Indochina." But "Hull notes" omitted any mention of [225]Manchuria or part of China already colonized by Japan and had no deadline for troop withdrawal as well. Therefore this was not an "ultimatum" that might cause fatal damage to the Japanese empire and its hegemony. Hideki Tojo could have understood it as an "ultimatum" due to his narrow-mindedness, ignorance and lack of knowledge on diplomacy.

---

223   Herbert P. Bix Hirohito and the Making of Modern Japan pp. 478-429
224   Wikipedia: Kichisaburo Nomura. Online at http://en.wikipedia.org/wiki/Kichisaburo_Nomura
225   Wikipedia: Manchuria. Online at http://en.wikipedia.org/wiki/Manchuria

But there was no excuse for Shigenori Togo to interpret the document in this way. Many experts said, that as an accomplished diplomat he should have known it was not an "ultimatum." Probably, he intentionally misunderstood it because he was under a tremendous pressure from the camp of war advocates. Some of Togo's sympathizers argued that Togo had no choice but to sign a document to declare the war given the circumstances.

He did have a choice to resign, however, if he was truly against the war as people have the option to terminate his or her own career if it seems to demand criminal activities. Therefore, his responsibility for actions that led the nation into a tragic war was undeniable and so it is apparent that he deserved the 20 years prison sentence, although he appears to have had the noblest character among the 14 convicted prisoners.

One particular reason why Togo can be viewed more sympathetically than the other convicted Class-A War Criminals and that is by way of comparison of his treatment to that of Emperor Hirohito. American occupational forces excluded Hirohito from the Tokyo War Crime Trial and kept him on the throne, while it tried all other Japanese leaders who were in leadership when war broke. [226]General Douglas MacArthur (1880-1964) decided to keep Hirohito because he found Hirohito useful to reform Japan's political system, and was afraid of possible socio-political complications that dethroning him would cause. He thought that keeping Hirohito on the throne would maintain peaceful transition to a democratic Japan as an occupation force was in place. But it is difficult to see that Hirohito's responsibility was lighter than Togo's.

There were two additional people enshrined in Yasukuni. They were tried, but not convicted, because they died due to illness before a judicial decision was reached. [227]Admiral Osami Nagano (永野修身) (1880–1947) was a prominent leader of the Imperial Japanese Navy before and during the Second World

---

226   Wikipedia: Douglas MacArthur. Online at http://en.wikipedia.org/wiki/Douglas_
       MacArthur
227   Wikipedia: Osami Nagano. Online at http://en.wikipedia.org/wiki/Osami_Nagano

War. Nagano was appointed Minister of the Navy under Prime Minister Koki Hirota in 1936, and was appointed Commander in Chief of entire Japanese Fleet in 1937.

In 1941, Nagano became Chief of the Naval General Staff. In this capacity, Nagano adopted Admiral Isoroku Yamamoto's (山本五十六) (1884–1943) plan of attack against the United States Pacific Fleet in Pearl Harbor, in case diplomatic negotiations failed and Japan and the United States went to war. He supported the decision to wage war against the United States, Great Britain and the Netherlands. Nagano subsequently ordered the attack on Pearl Harbor. Nagano was promoted to fleet admiral in 1943 and kept his position as Chief of the Naval General Staff throughout the majority of the Second World War.

After the battle of Midway, Japan had suffered serious military setbacks and Nagano had lost the confidence of Emperor Hirohito. With the emperor's approval, Prime Minister Hideki Tojo and Navy Minister Shigetaro Shimada (1883–1976) removed Nagano from his post and replaced him with Shimada. Nagano spent the remainder of the war as an adviser to the government. Arrested by the American Occupation forces in 1945, Nagano, while standing before the International Military Tribunal on "Class-A" war criminal charges, assumed responsibility for the Pearl Harbor attack. Nagano died of a heart attack due to complications arising from pneumonia in Sugamo Prison in Tokyo before the conclusion of the trial in 1947.

[228]Yosuke Matsuoka (松岡洋右) (1880–1946) was a Foreign Minister of Japan shortly before the Second World War. Born in Japan in 1880, Yosuke Matsuoka traveled to the United States as a teenager and eventually studied law at the University of Oregon, from which he graduated in 1900. During his stay, he was a fervent Christian who attended Bible sessions at his high school and met the American Populist William Jennings Bryan (1860 –1925). Matsuoka eventually returned to Japan and joined the Foreign Service, which he served in for eighteen

---

228   Wikepedia: Yosuke Matsuoka. Online at http://en.wikipedia.org/wiki/Yosuke_
       Matsuoka

years. In 1940, Matsuoka became Minister of Foreign Affairs under Prime Minister Fumimaro Konoe (1891–1945).

Matsuoka was a major advocate of a Japanese alliance with Nazi Germany and Fascist Italy, whose assistance he saw as a perfect balancing force against the United States, and as such was one of the primary individuals who orchestrated the [229]*Tripartite Pact* in 1940.

Matsuoka also signed a Russo-Japanese non-aggression treaty in April 1941. However, after Germany's invasion of the Soviet Union in June 1941, Hitler proposed to Matsuoka that Japan take part in the attack as well. Matsuoka became a fervent supporter of the idea that Japan attack Russia and constantly pressured Konoe leaders of the Imperial Japanese Army and thte Imperial Japanese Navy to mobilize the military for that purpose.

Despite the military's opposition to his ideas, Matsuoka continued to loudly advocate an invasion of Russia and became increasingly reckless in his diplomatic dealings with the United States, who Matsuoka believed was conspiring to provoke Japan into a war. Matsuoka's hostility towards the U.S. who were vocal opponents of Japan's military campaigns, alarmed Konoe, who wanted to avoid war with the United States. Konoe and the military hierarchy conspired to get rid of Matsuoka. To this end, Konoe resigned in July 1941 and his cabinet ministers resigned with him, including Matsuoka. Konoe immediately was made prime minister again, and replaced Matsuoka as Foreign Minister with Admiral Teijiro Toyoda (1885-1961). Matsuoka subsequently drifted into obscurity. Captured by the Allies in 1945 and brought up on war crimes charges by the International Military Tribunal, Matsuoka died in 1946 before his trial was completed. His name is amongst the so-called 14 Class-A war criminals who are enshrined at Yasukuni Shrine despite never having been convicted. In 1979, Emperor Hirohito expressed his displeasure with the enshrinement of Matsuoka as well as Shiratori.

---

229   Wikepedia: Tripartite Pact. Online at http://en.wikipedia.org/wiki/Tripartite_Pact

It is a sad fact that Matsuoka, who once accepted Christ in his youth during his study in the States and was once a passionate believer, ended up as a the strong ally of Nazi Germany, a Class-A War criminal and a Kami in Yasukuni. Hirohito's comments indicate that Matsuoka was not good enough even for Yasukuni's Kami. There was no way to explain why such tragic fall happened to him in his later years while he was at one time a born again believer. No one will be able to answer to this question except our sovereign God.

Going back to the topic of Tojo and Togo, [230]Cordell Hull (1871–1955), one of the Nobel Laureates of 1945 and the United States Secretary of State who negotiated with the Japanese government for peace in the Pacific Region before the war broke out in 1941, [231]described Hideki Tojo as a "typical Japanese (army) officer, with a small-bore, straight-laced, one-track mind." He was "stubborn and self-willed, rather stupid, hard-working, and possessed a quantity of drive." He also referred to Shigenori Togo in his 1948 autobiography as "typical Japanese Foreign Office official, a good technician in his craft but also rather narrow in his views and unable to gain a broad perspective."

Hull's view on General Tojo was negative except for his work ethics, i.e., "quantity of drive" which was also recognized by Sadao Akamatsu. Hull did not view Tojo as a dictator like Hitler but neither as a suitable person for a leadership position of an important nation. Hull's observation seemed to parallel Isamu Taniguchi's view regarding Tojo's weakness that he was narrow-minded and lacked objective judgments due to his strong opinions and feelings toward certain persons and matters. Tojo's crime to have conscripted Toneo Nakamura and Shigeyoshi Matsumae made them lowest rank soldiers and send them to battle fields could be seen to be planned by his subordinates but not so much by Tojo himself as he was not smart enough to be a devil, according to Hull and Taniguchi. He was still guilty, however, of

230   Wikipedia: Cordell Hull. Online at http://en.wikipedia.org/wiki/Cordell_Hull
231   Cordell Hull. The Memoirs of Cordell Hull. (London, UK: Hodder & Stoughton, 1948; reprint, Temecula CA.: Reprint Services Corp, 1993)

the crime of listening and following an evil one, although he was not a devil himself. Tojo was guilty for the failure to control his subordinates in the same way Hirohito was guilty for failing to control Tojo and allowing the war to start.

Hull also viewed Togo as a person with some serious defects as a leader and diplomat, although a much better person than Tojo. Also, contrary to Bix, Hull viewed Hirohito as a mere "figurehead under the control of the military Cabinet." When President Franklin D. Roosevelt was looking for an option to send a message directly to Hirohito, Hull remarked it might aggravate the circumstance or be futile at best, because the emperor did not have the real power to start or to stop the war. Hull suggested that Roosevelt should therefore regard the message to Hirohito as the last recourse.

Only the Emperor Exonerated

When the war ended, [232]MacArthur gave only Emperor Hirohito among all Japanese leaders complete immunity, while the rest of them went on trial. It seems extremely odd that only Hirohito had no sentence, no trial in the court or was not even prosecuted simply because General Douglas MacArthur of the American occupational forces gave him a complete exemption from being subject to trial as a war criminal in order to rewrite his wartime record. I'm certain that if Hirohito deserved immunity from prosecution, Togo deserved it even more. Then, if Togo had a 20 year sentence, Hirohito deserved 30 years or more. In other words, Hirohito carried more guilt than Togo, though other critics don't view him as guilty as Tojo.

In my personal view, the double standard of giving immunity only to Emperor Hirohito was the greatest mistake Gen. MacArthur made. It created a very cloudy historical memory among the Japanese people. In later chapters there will be more discussion on the role of Hirohito in pre Second World War Japan, his deeds and his responsibility.

---

232   Joseph Huang. HIROHITO, MASTERMIND OF JAPANESE INVOLVEMENT IN WWII. Online at http://hope-of-israel.org/hirohito.htm

[233] Hirohito & Douglas MacArthur, 1945.[234]

---

233   Was available August 2010: http://ww2db.com/image.php?image_id=843
234   The picture is used under "fair dealing" (Canada) and "fair use" (USA)
      provisions in copyright law.

CHAPTER 7

KOKUTAI: THE CULTIC COMMUNITY OF THE EMPEROR

[235]*Kokutai* (Kyūjitai: 國體, Shinjitai: 国体, lit. national essence/entity/polity) was an ideological system and "moral concept that constituted the very essence of the state" that the Meiji Government invented around the emperor system. The word *Kokutai* was formed by two *kanji*. One of them, 国 *koku* meant "country," and the other 体 *tai* meant "body" or "shape." The precise definition of the term simply meant "shape of the country," but depending on the period of time and those who interpreted the word, it was understood in many different ways.

Ultranationalists in Japan believed that it was a framework for the true understanding of what was Japanese. It was the ideological system based on the supreme authority of the emperor as the inviolable high priest or spiritual head of the nation. The national government employed the system without questioning starting from the promulgation of the Meiji Constitution in 1889 until the final defeat of the nation in 1945. In this ideological system, the entire state was a unitary sacro-society or form of cultic religious community that involved the emperor, government and all citizens or subjects of the country.

Ritsuryo System & Kokutai

[236]The concept of *Kokutai* was modeled after a sacro-religious community named *Ritsuryo* System, created by Prince Shotoku (574-622) who was born as the son of Emperor Yōmei

---

235   Wikipedia: Kokutai. Online at http://en.wikipedia.org/wiki/Kokutai
236   Joseph Kitagawa. The Japanese Kokutai (National Community) History and Myth. History of Religions, 1974 p. 219

and fervently introduced Chinese writing system to Japan. In the 19th Century, Meiji oligarchy modified the system, incorporating many Western thoughts and a newly created emperor centered ideology into it. Shotoku ruled as the regent under his aunt, Empress Suiko (554–628) who was quick to recognize the need of a national community with a centralized government instead of a collection of barbaric tribes. The intentions of both Suiko and Shotoku were transforming primitive Japan ruled by warlords or tribal kings into a unified nation-state modeled after China with a far more advanced governing system than their country. Inspired by the Chinese Emperor [237]Wen (541-604) of [238]*Sui Dynasty*, Shotoku incorporated Confucianism and Buddhism into the Japanese indigenous Shinto ceremony and created *Ritsuryo*, a unique sacro-religious system in which Shinto based ceremonial rituals and politics became one.

According to [239]Thomas P. Kaslis, the justification of the Imperial system by Prince Shotoku was the strong synchronization of Shinto, Confucianism and Buddhism. First, the Shinto myth in *Kojiki* and *Nihonshoki* established the divine lineage of the Imperial family. Kaslis noted that as Shotoku established the Ritsuryo system, he incorporated Confucian based ruling principle of a nation and code of appropriate behavior as well as the philosophy.

Ritsuryo & Cultural Revolution

[240]One important theme central to Confucianism that Japanese rulers adopted was that of relationships, and the differing duties arising from the different status one held in relation to others. Individuals were expected to manage different degrees of relationship with different people, namely, as a junior in relation to their parents and elders, and as a senior in relation to their younger siblings, students, and others. In today's Japanese language, there is a distinction between

---

237   Wikipedia: Emperor Wen of Sui. Online at http://en.wikipedia.org/wiki/Emperor_ Wen_of_Sui
238   Wikipedia: Sui Dynasty. Online at http://en.wikipedia.org/wiki/Sui_Dynasty
239   Thomas P Kasulis. Shinto --- The Way Home (Honolulu, USA: University of Hawaii Press, 2004) pp. 86-90
240   Wikipedia: Confucianism. Online at http://en.wikipedia.org/wiki/Confucian

the way juniors address seniors and the way seniors address juniors. Also, in most work settings workers must address their superiors in the same way juniors address their seniors no matter how old they are. Even among college students, there is a distinction between senpai (先輩) or senior students and kohai or junior students. Senpai is a student who enters the school before kohai (後輩) and sometimes younger than kohai. However, he or she must be honored by kohai and addressed in the same way as younger people address older people. In some sports clubs, the distinction is extremely intense and Senpai treat kohai almost like a slave. Some new students die from alcohol poisoning each year during the welcome party to the collage sports teams, as they are offered an extraordinary quantity of sake or beer to drink by the senpai students and fail to decline the offer.

The custom of social hierarchy deeply rooted in Japanese society might have stemmed from the Confucian social ethics or the philosophy of Filial piety to differentiate juniors and seniors, superiors and inferiors, to differentiate people groups based on the social hierarchies. The philosophy of Filial piety, introduced to Japan from China during the reign of Prince Shotoku, was an important factor in the nation's governance. It was considered among the greatest of virtues and must be shown towards both the living and the dead. The term "filial", meaning "of a child", denoted the respect and obedience of a child shown to his parents, especially to his father. The principle of Filial piety was an extremely vital part of Ritsuryo System because it taught the nation the duty of loyalty to the emperor with divine lineage.

Also, as a devout Buddhist, Shotoku intended to introduce Buddhist ethics to discourage conflicts, civil strives and murders or even slaughters of animal for food, so that he could govern the nation more peacefully. He emphasized the inner life and personal cultivation based on Buddhism. Shotoku was a dedicated Buddhist himself who believed that the ruler should have compassion for people and fairness to all and that loyal subjects should use Buddhist practices to achieve an egoless commitment to national harmony. The Japanese vegetarian diet also started around the eighth century, since Buddhism discouraged the consumption of animal's meat. Many meat based recipes disappeared from the archipelago at this time. The Ritsuryo system that Shotoku created was designed to reform the Japanese social-psychological scheme of the nation as well as the political scene. It brought a great [241]cultural revolution comparable with the one that China's Chairman [242]Mao Zedong (1893–1976) did in 1966 as Shotoku introduced these new philosophies into the primitive and illiterate nation.

After Shotoku's death, Japan became a highly centralized state nation modeled after the imperial model of China during the *Sui* Dynasty. Japan's indigenous *Kami* were somehow blended with Taoism deities, which also immigrated into Japan with Buddhism and Confucianism. These made an assumption that the authority of the emperor was destined to reign over the nation, because he was descended from the Sun Goddess Amaterasu. Confucianism was applied to control offices of the government by imposing bureaucratic hierarchies and a strict chain of command over workers. During the seventh century, the religio-political structure developed on the basis of Shinto-Confucianism-Buddhism syncretism.

The emperor's power faded in the late 12th century, but the Fujiwara clan and Samurai class rulers continued to use the system with minor modifications. These rulers conveniently used the system and the state running philosophy beyond what Shotoku created for centuries by synchronizing Shinto, Buddhism.

After a period of long dormancy of the emperor's power, the ruling class people during the Meiji era created a new system based on the old Ritsuryo. The new system was more aggressive and highlighted the assumption that the emperor was divine. It was very militaristic primarily because the Meiji Oligarchy added the fourth element, the Enlightenment philosophy from the West or a type of cultural Viagra into the older system composed

---

241   Wikipedia: Cultural Revolution. Online at http://en.wikipedia.org/wiki/Cultural_
      Revolution
242   Wikipedia: Mao Zedong. Online at http://en.wikipedia.org/wiki/Mao_Zedong

of Shinto, Buddhism and Confucianism. The older system that Shotoku created was more balanced and benign than this militaristic modern version of Kokutai, although the system was still based on the assumption that Japanese emperor came from the divine lineage of Amaterasu.

The new Kokutai professed that the emperor was a divine despot in the same sense as the Roman Caesar was proclaimed prior to the Christian era. Incorporation of the Western modernism or the philosophy of the Enlightenment[243] into Prince Shotoku's Ritsuryo system into the Meiji Government created the new Kokutai out of an ancient mummy that resembled [244]Frankenstein's "monster." The monster created in the biomechanical lab of the Meiji oligarchy ruled the nation with an iron fist and transformed it into what seemed like a power hungry, bloodthirsty warmonger. On the other hand, Prince Shotoku's Ritsuryo system brought a great cultural revolution, which reformed the psychological structure of the nation as well as the political domain. However, the only cultural and socio-psychological contribution that the new Kokutai had was the creation and enforcement of the extremely militaristic ideology like Islamic fundamentalism to hold the divinity of the emperor. The new ideology after the Meiji era was nothing more than a psychoactive stimulant to produce delusions and grandiose fantasy about the Great Imperial Japan and deprived the whole nation of the sense of reality.

Modernized Kokutai under Meiji Constitution

In the 19th Century, Meiji Restorationists revived the over 1,000 year old *Ritsuryo,* religio-political system and recreated it into a governing system of a nation-state in a modern era. They also synchronized some Western philosophies or political ideologies from Europe mainly developed in the era of the Enlightenment into Prince Shotuku's 1,300 years old system. In the process when the draft of Meiji constitution was created, there was a heated debate between the liberals and conservatives. Liberals

---

243   Wikipedia: Enlightenment (concept). Online at http://en.wikipedia.org/wiki/
      Enlightenment_%28concept%29
244   Wikipedia: Frankenstein. Online at http://en.wikipedia.org/wiki/Frankenstein

held the view that the constitution should include only Seitai or a governing system, but not Kokutai or any mythologically based sacro-religious system. Conservatives, however, insisted that they the constitution must stipulate the Kokutai model built on the medieval Ritsuryo system as the national essence of the nation-state.

[245]Fukuzawa Yukichi (福澤諭吉)[246] (1830-1901), one of proponents of the liberal view, contended that almost everyone agreed that Japan's National Essence was unique because of the unbroken succession of Emperors begun by the oath of the Sun Goddess Amaterasu. But he made clear that this did not constitute the National Essence itself. The unparalleled succession of Emperors could be used to promote Japan's national sovereignty, not by stipulating it in the constitution, but by using it to focus the sentiments of the people. Fukuzawa insisted that the constitution must stipulate only *Seitai* (政体) or the governing style, but not *Kokutai*, or national community in a spiritual dimension.

As a rational scientific thinker with some Western education, Fukuzawa did not believe in the teachings that the Meiji government propagated, including the divinity of the emperor. But he he did not profess this doubt in public. In an unofficial memo between approximatley 1875 to 1877, however, Fukuzawa wrote, "The holy Son of Heaven of blessed reign is a falsehood. In modern times, Emperors and Shoguns have been nobodies." He was far apart from the ideological Meiji Restorationist of his day who believed in the ancient myths about the emperors throughout history and the imperial family or lineage as the literal truth. He did, however, recognize the practical value of maintaining such ideas as means to promote Japan's national sovereignty.

---

245   Wikepedia: Fukuzawa Yukichi. Online at http://en.wikipedia.org/wiki/Fukuzawa_Yukichi

246   John S. Brownlee. Four Stages of Japanese Kokutai. JSAC Conference, University of British Columbia, October 2000. Online at http://www.iar.ubc.ca/centres/cjr/seminars/semi2000/jsac2000/brownlee.pdf

[247]In 1880, Japan moved toward a constitutional govern- ment under the Emperor as sovereign in the state, but Fukuzawa's liberal position was washed away. As [248]Okuma Shigenobu (大隈重信) (1838-1922), a liberal among the leaders of the Meiji government and Fukuzawa's close ally was ousted; conservatives immediately took control of drafting the constitution. The court noble and a super-conservative among Meiji Oligarchy, [249]Iwakura Tomomi (岩倉具視) (1825-83) laid out principles for a draft constitution by the Council of State:

1. The Constitution shall emanate from the Emperor and the policy of a gradual approach toward constitutitonal government shall prevail.

2. The Emperor shall have supreme command over the army and navy, declare war, make peace, conclude treaties, etc.; moreover, the Emperor will direct the national administration.

3. The organization of the cabinet shall not be subjected to the intervention of parliament.

[250]For Iwakura, *Kokutai* was literally the national essence of the country coming from his ancestors, and therefore must be preserved forever. He maintained that countries where the Kokutai changed, or was unstable, violated the way of Heaven and Earth. The principles were established everywhere and forever, of the unbroken succession of emperors for ages eternal, of affectionate relations between father and son, and of the duties of the ruler and the subjects, resulting in the prosperous country of the present day. In other words, Iwakura viewed the

---

247   Brownlee. Four Stages of Japanese Kokutai. JSAC Conference, University of British Columbia.
248   Wikipedia: Ōkuma Shigenobu. Online at http://en.wikipedia.org/wiki/Okuma_ Shigenobu
249   Wikipedia: Iwakura Tomomi. Online at http://en.wikipedia.org/wiki/Iwakura_ Tomomi
250   Brownlee. Four Stages of Japanese Kokutai. JSAC Conference, University of British Columbia.

principles of *Kokutai*, unbroken succession of emperors and his rules were a deontological "eternal must" that existed in the metaphysical world from the eternal past and did not change from the very beginning.

Iwakura portrayed himself as the defender of the eternal Kokutai coming from his ancestors. However, his logic seemed to be modeled after [251]Kantian metaphysics from the West, which postulated the transcendental idealism with the eternal law in the "noumenal realm." The real Ritsuryo system inherited from Prince Shotoku and other ancestors had never postulated the concept of the *Eternal Kokutai* in the metaphysical *a priori* world as did the one of [252]Immanuel Kant (1724–1804) the author of [253]*Critique of Pure Reason* (1781). Iwakura declared that his country must remain purely Japanese following 1,300 years of tradition inherited from his ancestors. However, either knowingly or unknowingly, he had incorporated 1,300 years old traditional thinking with Western philosophies in an extremely destructive manner.

[254]D.C. Holtom (1963) maintains that numerous Japanese scholars in the Meiji era including those from Shinto schools insisted that their State Shinto was not a genuine religion since it was under the supervision of the government. He also noted that few Japanese statesmen during the early Meiji period were more liberal and possessed better common sense than Iwakura and other State Shinto proponents among the ruling class during the same era. Quoting one of the most influential Post-Second World War Japanese authorities on Shinto, Holtom contends that:

> A nonreligious status was clamed for the state cult
> by the Meiji statesmen in order to avoid a head-
> on collision with Christianity, which at the time

251   Wikipedia: Kantianism. Online at http://en.wikipedia.org/wiki/Kantianism
252   Wikipedia: Immanuel Kant. Online at http://en.wikipedia.org/wiki/Immanuel_
       Kant
253   Immanuel Kant. Critique of Pure Reason, Abridged. (Indianapolis, IN: Hackett
       Publishing C ompany, 1781/1999)
254   D.C. Holtom. Modern Japan and Shinto Nationalism. (New York, USA: Paragon
       Book Reprint Corp, 1963) p. 39

had the support of Western nations that Japan
could not afford to offend (Holtom, 1963).

According to Holtom, Japan's liberal statesmen with better
common sense like Fukuzawa and Okuma were afraid of giving an
impression to the Western nations that Japan had transformed
into a dangerous community of cult centered on the emperor
from a feudal nation ruled by the Shogunate. Japan could not
afford to offend the Westerners who held to Christian ethics
since they needed large amount of aid and support from the
West to continue the modernization and technological upgrade
of the country.

After the expulsion of Okuma, nobody in the government
had a progressive mindset to promote a democratic constitution
or to raise serious questions about the new *Kokutai* system
they were constructing, though many among the intelligentsia
and the general public did. [255]According to John Brownlee
(2000), the newly created modern version of *Kokutai* from the
Meiji Restoration to 1945, served as an inspiring and unifying
ideology, and provided the national political framework within
which to place the system of a constitutional monarchy modeled
after the West under the Meiji Constitution.

The system worked effectively for a while to unify the nation
and give an adrenalin shot to the Japanese psyche. The Kokutai
system, however, went wrong and turned out to be the system
of oppression after a series of wars against its neighbors, since
it was modeled after Western imperialism. As Japan continued
Imperialistic military expenditure, Kokutai became a bloodthirsty
monster which continued to grow, feeding on soldiers' flesh and
blood.

With the promulgation of the Meiji Constitution in 1889, the
emperor's divinity and undisputable inviolability was stipulated,
but not the details of his divine origin. [256]As the emperor was

---

255   Brownlee. Four Stages of Japanese Kokutai. JSAC Conference, University of
      British Columbia.
256   Brownlee. Four Stages of Japanese Kokutai. JSAC Conference, University of
      British Columbia

declared sovereign because of his descent in a line unbroken for ages eternal, as well sacred and inviolable, the essential conditions were established for the preservation of the *Kokutai*. The mythologically oriented divine founding of the country and of the imperial house during the age of the gods provided the ultimate justification for the *Kokutai*. This divine founding of the country was not mentioned at all in the constitution. It was, however, understood by everyone and taught as historical truth in Japan's educational system, from elementary schools through universities, until 1945.

According to [257]Tatsukichi Minobe (1873-1948), *Kokutai* was understood as the "shape of the Estate" in the sense of emperor as the "organ of the Estate," while *Kokutai* was given a mystical power. The emperor was a "god among humans," the incarnation of the national morals. However, the conservatives were furious about Minobe's more logical and rational interpretation of the system, since his notion denied the supernatural and mystical power that the system possessed. *Kokutai* for the conservative in the era Minobe lived, was something extra-juridical, supernatural and something like religious dogma or a black box in which followers of a certain cult group were not allowed to ask about the content. [258]Joseph Kitagawa (1973) described Kokutai created by the Meiji Government as the combination of mythologization of history and historization of myth. Therefore Kokutai imposed the belief of both mythologized history and historized myth simultaneously on the citizens of Japan.

[259]Josefa Valderrama López (2006) promotes the idea that the system of *Kokutai* represented the concept of *kazoku kokka* or the state as a family or household. This implied the idea that the *Kokutai* was a system constructed upon the as-sumption that the emperor's family was the head of all families in Japan. The government created the ideological formula of the "Family Estate" (家族国家 kazoku kokka), a mechanism through

---

257   Wikipedia: Minobe Tatsukichi. Online at http://en.wikipedia.org/wiki/Minobe_Tatsukichi
258   Joseph Kitagawa. The Japanese Kokutai (National Community) History and Myth. History of Religions, 1974 p. 226
259   López. Beyond words: the "kokutai" and its background, 2006.

which the *Kokutai* and the perfection of the emperor centered worldview were explained. The emperor was the foundation of the nation-state which represented the spirits of the ancestors of the Japanese race and therefore, he was the sovereign of the state, like a "head of the family" incarnation of the authority of the ancestors of the clan with the patriarchal power on the family group.

In summary, *Kokutai* was an ideological system and "moral concept that constituted the very essence of the state" that the leaders of Meiji Government created. It essentially followed the same principle as the Prince Shotoku's religio-political system named Ritsuryo, but there were some essential differences. For instance, in Prince Shotoku's system, the emperor had some divine attributes being descended from Amaterasu the Sun Goddess. Therefore he was occasionally treated as *Kami* or *Arahitogami* (divine man). However, he was not classified as a god or all-powerful deity in a regular Western sense. It was a creation of the Meiji Oligarchy by amalgamating Prince Shotoku's Ritsuryo system inherited from the antiquity and Western modernism during the era of the Enlightenment.

The model in which the emperor was a sacred and inviolable deity and the powerful head of the state at the same time seemed to be modeled after the religio-political system in the ancient [260]Rome rather than more harmless and graceful Prince Shotoku's system. As Kitagawa stated Meiji Government imposed Japanese citizens to believe the combination of mythologization of history and historization of myth, they were forced to accept *Kokutai* literally as the national essence of the country coming from his ancestors, or deontological "eternal must," deemed to preserve forever.

So the creation of the Meiji government grew into a horrific monster by the early 20th century. The audacious dream of

---

260   From the Meiji Restoration (1868) to the end of the World War II (1945), Japan had same kind of madness as Rome. The nation was extremely aggressive, impudent, and militaristic, did not tolerate any contradiction with emperor-centered *Kokutai*.

the Japanese militarists who attempted to extend the imperial rule over the entire East Asia, failed in 1945 when Japan gave unconditional surrender to the Allied Forces. As Emperor Hirohito renounced his divinity of sovereignty after the Second World War, the Japanese National Community officially lost a paradigm that had been sustained for generations.

Non-Shinto Religions & Kokutai

[261]Akira Kurihara (1990) also noted that some non-Shinto religious organizations supported the emperor worship and Kokutai system. They were called the "Japanese national religions," *Nihon minzoku shukyo*. These religious organizations were not State Shinto, but embraced the mentality that supported the Japanese emperor cult. It was a concept that widely embraced such things as Kokutai or national polity, Japanism (Nihonshugi), spiritualism (seishinshugi), and "crisis ethos" (hijyo no seishin). Kurihara called these religious organizations "new religions" and continued his discussion that:

> [262]Tosaka pointed out the trinity that supported the Japanese national religion: the military, government officialdom, and "Big Bourgeoisie, Japan-style." At the same time he says that, supported by this trinity, the Japanese national religion penetrated into all spheres of life: education, folklore, literature, the arts, and even politics and economics. In other words, the ultimate attainment of the emperor system was to be the religion of everyday life, to be an emperor system at work in everyday consciousness. This, according to Tosaka, is what the Japanese national religion was all about (Kurihara, 1990).

[263]Kurihara also noted that Examples of New Religions

---

261   Akira Kurihara. Emperor System as National Religion. Japanese journal of Religious Studies, 1990 p. 317

262   Jun Tosaka. Shiso to Fuzoku [Thought and customs]. Reprinted in Tosaka Jun senshu, vol 4. (Tokyo: Ito Shoten, 1936)

263   Akira Kurihara. Emperor System as National Religion. Japanese journal of Religious Studies, 1990 p. 317

which emerged around this time were the *Hito-no-michi*, the *Dainihon Kannonkai* (later named *Sekai Kyaseikyo*), the *Oomotokyo*, and the *Reiyiikai*. Some religious organizations not classified as Shinto embraced vital components of Kokutai or emperor-centered cultic community, teaching rites supportive of the emperor's divinity. In 1940 Prime Minister Kiichiro Hiranuma's government enacted the most evil [264]Religious Organization Law in Japan's history. Under this law, the government had power to control all religious organizations like other corporations or companies. These non-Shinto religions practicing "emperor cult" became officially recognized religions under the law. If they did not comply with the government policy to enforce the emperor worship, they were banned to practice all official religious activities, having lost the legal status as religious organizations.

After the defeat in the war, as government's control over religious organizations ceased to exist, the emperor's semi-divine status was denied. The non-Shinto religious organizations stopped professing the emperor's divinity, since it was not required any more. Yet, many of these groups still gave the emperor and imperial family very high esteem, revered and honourable position as the spiritual symbol of the Japanese nation.

End of Kokutai & Retention of Emperor System

For Japanese leaders from the Meiji Restoration to the end of the war *Kokutai* or emperor centered ideological system was more important than even their own lives. In the summer of 1945, [265]Japan's defeat in the World War II appeared inevitable after losing more than the half of the combined fleet during the series of battles. However, the leaders there could not simply surrender because the safety of the emperor and the imperial institution were not guaranteed in the Allied demand for unconditional surrender. They did not seek immunity for themselves as leaders

---

264   O'Brien and Ohsaki. To dream of dreams : religious freedom and constitutional politics in postwar Japan, p. 46
265   Brownlee. Four Stages of Japanese Kokutai. JSAC Conference, University of British Columbia.

or safety for the people of Japan. They only wanted a guarantee for the survival of the imperial household, in which the *Kokutai* was incarnate.

After these leaders finally made a decision to surrender to the Allied Force, *Kokutai* as a state was dismantled. Though the imperial system was sustained and the emperor's household survived, it was reduced to a ceremonial position. This was because General Douglas MacArthur (1880–1964) of the American occupational forces thought the monarchy was useful as a tool to obtain a consensus and the cooperation of the Japanese public as he reformed Japan's political system.

In Japan's post Second World War constitution, the emperor was strictly a ceremonial monarchy defined as symbol of a nation-state with no political authority or spiritual significance in the Shinto religion. Many conservative politicians, however, still viewed the emperor as Japan's spiritual leader even without political power, since they had inherited the religio-spiritual tradition from pre-Second World War politics.

[266]Kitagawa raised the last question in his journal article, "whether or not such a paradigm still survived in the minds of the people in the unconscious realm of the National Community is still another question." Japan had a new constitution that denied the divinity of the emperor or any form of state religion after 1945. Although the average Japanese after the war did not care for the emperor-centered ideology and spiritual system at all, the nation's conservative leaders were constantly waiting for chances to revive the older paradigm. The conservatives believed that the old emperor-centered ideological system was still alive in the unconscious realm of the Japanese.

Surprisingly, the emperor system was preserved, mainly because General [267]MacArthur decided not to terminate it after the war. Many inside and outside of the country raised concerns

---

266   Joseph Kitagawa. The Japanese Kokutai (National Community) History and
       Myth. History of Religions, 1974 p. 226
267   Douglas MacArthur was an American army general who oversaw the
       occupation of Japan from 1945 to 1951 and is credited for making far-ranging
       democratic changes in that country.

KOKUTAI: THE CULTIC COMMUNITY OF THE EMPEROR 123

regarding resuscitation of the past seeming monster that ruled the nation during more than a century prior to the end of the war. Since the Meiji Government had a history of resuscitating the 1,700 year old Ritsuryo system back to life in the 19th century and recreating it into a gigantic totalitarian, psycho-spiritual ruling system which caused the total destruction of the Japanese nation before the mid-nineteenth century, one could not 100 percent deny the possibility that *Kokutai*, a seeming prehistoric monster might come back to life.

Creation of State Shinto – very powerful spiritual force

Prior to the Meiji period, the Shinto religion was strictly an animistic folk religion closely tied to the annual agricultural rites and other festivities. Shinto was simply a public ceremonial religion with a rich variety of annual agricultural rites deeply rooted in the daily life of Japanese people, and most of them were associated with harvest rites from the ancient time. It was a non-ideological religion only associated with the daily routine of life and completely foreign from Imperialistic Nationalism and an Emperor Cult, though the emperor was revered as the high priest who performed the agricultural rites.

However, after the Meiji Restoration, a new type of Shinto as a part of ideological system centered on the emperor came into existence. To establish the Shinto Religion as a state cult, the leadership of the Meiji government had to transform Shinto doctrine to be compatible with their ideology. [268]D.C. Holtom maintained that the Meiji oligarchy had to deal with problems within Shinto itself. One of these problems, according to Holtom, was the elimination of nonofficial interpretations of the foundational stories stated in *Kojiki* and *Nihonshoki*. In order to accomplish this end, the authority of the government made a bold attempt to create two categories of the Shinto Religion. It was a form of genetic engineering separating *Kokka Shinto* or State Shinto and *Shuha Shinto* or Sectarian Shinto. The

---

268   D.C. Holtom. Modern Japan and Shinto Nationalism, New York: USA Paragon
       Book Reprint Corp, 1963) p.28

latter was allowed to exist in the same way as other religions just as Christianity and Buddhism under the Meiji Constitution that guaranteed freedom of religious faith with limitations. The former, however, was considered to represent the true and uncontaminated line of pure Shinto and protected in a special status because of its value to the state.

When the Meiji Constitution was promulgated in 1889, State Shinto was rather more ceremonial than the agency to indoctrinate the nation because liberals like Fukuzawa and Okuma had some power to influence the government. [269]Holtom noted that the priests of the State shrines were prohibited from attempting to indoctrinate parishioners with any tenets of belief. Their chief functions were supposed to be those rituals and ceremonies to protect the state. But as time passed and liberal influence to the government faded and then eliminated almost completely, State Shinto became able to control and rule with an iron fist.

The government and ruling class claimed that they had always been the "pure Shinto" from the era of Yamato, or the time Japan came into existence. Regarding the dogmas of nationalistic Shinto that Meiji Oligarchy created, [270]Holtom contends that:

> What is more, they are dogmas that are established
> and propagated by the unique power of the state
> itself. If any difference between Sectarian Shinto
> and State Shinto is to be drawn at this point, it
> is that the acceptance of the doctrines of the
> former is left to voluntary choice, while those
> of the latter are required by national authority
> as the essence of loyalty (Holtom, 1963).

In fact State Shinto was directly controlled by the government and possessed de facto power to rule national life. Priests were considered government officials and paid a salary from the

---

269   D.C. Holtom. Modern Japan and Shinto Nationalism, New York: USA Paragon
        Book Reprint Corp, 1963) p.32
270   D.C. Holtom. Modern Japan and Shinto Nationalism, New York: USA Paragon
        Book Reprint Corp, 1963) p.32

tax in the same way as clergies in contemporary socialist states. On the other hand, [271]Sectarian Shinto employed their own teachers, preachers and priests from their own funds coming from donations and offering. They were afforded the same legal treatment as Buddhism and Christianity, and maintained freedom and the independence from the State control. They carried on voluntary, nonofficial religious propaganda until the *Religious Organization Law* was enacted in 1940 under Prime Minister Kichiro Hiranuma's government. Under this law the government was able to control religious matter and every regulating religious organizations including Sectarian Shinto. All religious organizations had to apply for and be granted government recognition to operate legally, therefore they had to comply with the government accepting the teaching from the State Shinto and Emperor Cult.

Daijisai & Emperor Spirit

Regarding the meaning of *Daijosai* (大嘗祭), according to [272]Floyd Hiatt Ross it was the ceremony that their emperor in some deep sense became Kami (Ross, 1965). When *Daijosai* or the Grand Food Festival of New Food at Ascension was performed immediately after the ascension of a new emperor. Ross also noted that by performing this ritual, the emperor became emperor in fact as well as in name. It was a rite that the emperor officially became emperor by receiving the Emperor Spirit from his predecessor.

Joseph Kitagawa also maintained that the Japanese imperial institution did not depend on the moral virtues, superior learning or political abilities of the emperors as individuals. Instead, what made them emperors was *Tennorei* (天皇霊) or the"Imperial Spirit" transmitted throughout the ages.[273] The Imperial Spirit was transmitted to a new emperor during the feast of *Daijosai* or Ascension Rite. In other words, *Tennorei* was like a

271   D.C. Holtom. Modern Japan and Shinto Nationalism, New York: USA Paragon
       Book Reprint Corp, 1963) p.34
272   Floyd Hiatt Ross. Shinto The Way of Japan. (Boston, USA: Beacon Press,
       1965) 94
273   Joseph Kitagawa. Some Reflections and Its Relationship to the Imperial
       System. Journal of Religious Studies, 1990 p. 172

[274]*Trill Symbiont* in *StarTrek Universe*, a very long-lived or almost immortal slug-shaped entity that was hosted by a succession of humanoid species named *Trills*, a process called "joining." Each of the hosts had access to the memories of the previous hosts including the accumulated skills and work experiences. According to the belief of the emperor cult, the emperor was divine and inviolable because of this divine *Tennorei* or immortal Symbiont inside of his body. Hirohito as a person was merely a host in which the divine *Symbiont* resided. On his ascension to the throne, he then was to have received an immortal *Tennorei Symbiont* from his late father.

Hirohito's father [275]Yoshihito (嘉仁) or Emperor Taisho (大正天皇) (1879 – 1926), had poor health almost all his life and at times exhibited mental disability. As a young prince, Yoshihito contracted meningitis within three weeks of his birth that could have contributed to this physical and mental ill health. He entered the elementary department of the Gakushuin academy, but due to his health problems was often unable to continue his studies. Although he showed skill in some areas such as horse riding, he proved to be poor in areas requiring higher level thought. He was finally withdrawn from Gakushuin before finishing the middle school course in 1894. The only reason he inherited the throne from his father, the Great [276]Emperor Meiji (1852 – 1912) was because he was the only surviving male child in the family following the early death of his four older brothers. He was still revered and honored as the divine emperor after the ascension since he had the *Tennorei Symbiont* within. His moral virtues, lower than average intelligence, or his individual political abilities as an emperor did not matter because Yoshihito himself was simply the host in which the emperor spirit resided.

[277] Carman Blacker (1990) notes that the *Daijosai* was the oldest and most mysterious ceremony in the ritual sequence

274   Wikipedia: Dax (Star Trek). Online at http://en.wikipedia.org/wiki/Dax_ (Star_Trek)
275   Wikipedia: Emperor Taishō. Online at http://en.wikipedia.org/wiki/Taisho_ Emperor
276   Wikipedia: Emperor Meiji. Online at http://en.wikipedia.org/wiki/Emperor_Meiji
277   Carman Blacker. The Shinza or God-seat in the Daijosai – Throne, Bed or Incubation Couch? Japanese journal of Religious Studies, 1990

that marked the consecration of the Japanese emperor. The general purpose and intention of the ceremony of Daijisai was to enact symbolically the death of the new emperor to his old human state, and his rebirth as a divine or semi-divine being.

Blacker studied the significance of *Shinza* (神座) or the divine chair that was the most puzzling aspect of the ceremony of *Daijosai*. According to Blacker, it has been seen as a throne, as a marriage bed, a symbol of the Sun Goddess, a resting-place for a visiting god or a refuge where the emperor may receive the soul of his ancestors. Shinza was the central component of the whole sequence of the ceremony, which symbolized emperor's communion with Kami.

If the Shinza had the implication of marriage bed as Blacker noted, we could easily speculate the possibility of [278]Tantrism or ecstatic sexual unions between newly appointed emperor and divine hosts. [279]The development of Tantrism was traced from pre-Vedic times of India (roughly 1700 BCE and 600 BCE) through the Vedic, post-Vedic, early Buddhist and Jain periods and the practice of religio-sexual union between live humans and divine hosts that were widely spread into various religious communities all over the planet. [280]Robert Ellwood (1973) also didn't deny the possibility that the emperor slept with a female human host in which divinities resided during the ceremony in antiquity. But Blacker maintains that there is no evidence or written record to prove that the new emperor had sexual intercourse with a woman during Daijosai at least after the Meiji period.

In the ancient world, tantric religious rites of sexual unions between human subjects and spiritual beings were commonly practiced. In Ephesus, the temple of Artemis was the centre of tantric religions. It promoted sexual unions between humans and divine beings, holding many female temple prostitutes for interventions of these unions. In the New Testament the

---

278   Wikipedia: Tantra. Online at http://en.wikipedia.org/wiki/Tantrism

279   N. N. Bhattacharyya. History of the Tantric Religion: An Historical, Ritualistic, and Philosophical Study. (Columbia, MO: South Asia Books, 2006)

280   Robert S Ellwood. The Feast of Kingship: Ascension Ceremonies in Ancient Japan. Monumenta Nipponica Monographs 50. Tokyo: Sophia University, 1973 pp. 37-77

[281]Apostle Paul fiercely denounced tantric religion of Artemis when he visited Ephesus. He encountered angry riots of those who followed the cult of Artemis. These were led by a silversmith named Demetrius who made statues of the goddess for a living.

If the tantric rite of sexual unions was practiced in Daijosai, the emperor in antiquity could have sexual unions with both male and female Kami. Even without the intervention a human female host, having sex with spiritual beings was seeming obscene act controlled by the darkest part of the spiritual world. If any live human host who intervene these seeming obscene acts by having sex with a new emperor, it was tragic and made the history of Japanese Imperial family even worse.

[282]Blacker also notes that the climax of the rite was the communal meal. By eating the products of the earth with his ancestral Kami, the emperor acquired the magical power to bestow fertility on the land under his rule. Once he was divine, he had the right to eat *Ambrosia* or divine food with his divine hosts. Before he could reach this climactic moment of transformation, he must undergo a rite of passage. The necessary power must be conducted from the body of the old, dead emperor into his own body. To this end, he must revert to the condition of an embryo in the womb, wrapped in placenta. By this symbolic action he became the actual, direct child of Amaterasu.

Emperor System & Kokutai

Joseph Kitagawa contends that after the ascension of Hirohito upon the death of Taisho, the inviolable nature of emperorhood and the necessity of supreme patriotism to the throne and the nation quickly developed into a national cult. He states:

> The themes were repeated loudly and publicly on numerous occasions in the late 1920s and throughout the 1930s by all branches of the government (both

---

281   Acts 19
282   Carman Blacker. The Shinza or God-seat in the Daijosai – Throne, Bed or Incubation Couch? Japanese journal of Religious Studies, 1990 p. 188

national and prefectural), the army and navy, schools, and patriotic organizations. Throughout those years newspapers contained frequent reports of scholars, writers, and students, as well as religious figures and free thinkers, being sentenced on the charge of *Ikse mjestd*. The national atmosphere became particularly stifling in the 1930s as the authoritarian, militaristic, jingoistic, emotionally anti-foreign nationalists became increasingly more vocal and politically influential. (Kitagawa, 1991)

Kitagawa viewed that this system eventually led Japan to war. It controlled the media and oppressed freedom of speech within the whole country. The Cultic Community of *Kokutai* was becoming extremely lethal, powerful, undefeatable and unmanageable in the 1930s, and extended authoritarianism, militarism, and narcissistic anti-foreign nationalism to the whole nation.

In summary, the Ritsuryo System that Prince Shotoku created was a well-designed synchronization of Shinto, Confucianism and Buddhism and built the foundation of the nation-state of Japan. Although Ritsuryo was still the religio-political system of paganism from a Christian perspective, it was generally benign and beneficial to the public. It was also an innovative, ingenious and revolutionary style of ruling in those days. But the modern version of Kokutai that the Meiji Oligarchy created could be described as something like a God Worrior or Shishigami without head. It was a product of the hybridization of Prince Shotoku's Ritsuryo system and some Western models of dictatorial unitary sacro-societies like Pre-Christian Rome, in which the government and military of the divine emperor had absolute de facto force over the whole nation.

The leaders of the Meiji Government forged the Ritsuryo System and created a God Worrior or gigantic war machine, in the same way as Alberich the Nibelung dwarf in Richard Wagner's famous opera, [283]the Ring of the Niebelung (1854/1960) and

---

283   Richard Wagner. The Ring of the Nibelung. Translated, and with a foreword, by
      Stewart Robb. (NY: Dutton Press, 1854/1960)

group of elves in J. R. R. Tolkien's nobel [284]the Lord of the Rings (1954/2002) who transformed the Rhinegold into the Ring of Power. The sole reason of forging either the gold or ancient Japanese political system into whatever they wanted was the ceaseless lust for power and control. [285]Jean Shinoda Bolen (1992) contended that:

> To forge Rhinegold into an instrument of power
> that can be used to subjugate others is like tapping
> into this inner source of divinity and corrupting it.
> Charismatic and demonic leaders do this, and their
> followers become slaves to their leader's obsession for
> power and wealth. The Reverend James Jones, whose
> disciples followed him to their deaths in Jamestown,
> was such a leader, as was Hitler, who had an awesome
> mesmerizing aura at the height of his power.

[286] Sméagol (Gollum). The Lord of the Rings, 2001.[287]
Sméagol the Hobbit became obsessed with the
Ring that had eventually destroyed him.

---

284   J. R. R. Tolkien. The Lord of the Rings. (Boston, MA: Houghton Mifflin Press, 1954/2000)
285   Jean Shinoda Bolen. Ring of Power. (NY: HarperSanFrancisco, 1992) p. 37
286   Was available August 2010: http://images.search.yahoo.com/images
287   The picture is used under "fair dealing" (Canada) and "fair use" (USA) provisions in copyright law.

CHAPTER 8

RESUSCITATING THE EVIL GOD WARRIOR

Since the end of the Occupation, Japanese conservatives and underground movements led by a right-wing establishment have sought to restore State Shinto's institutions and the emperor centered *Kokutai* system. At that time, military budgets were expanded to the point that it placed Japan among the top five countries in defense spending. After the war, Japan's establishment and conservative *Liberal Democratic Party* (LDP) government periodically attempted to revive the power of the emperor system and Japan's prewar military presence.

Series of Attempts to Restore Japan's Stare Shinto

The movement to restore Japan's State Shinto after the Second World War began to get attention from the media and encounter both foreign and domestic protest after [288]Prime Minister Yasuhiro Nakasone's (中曽根康弘) (born 1918) official visit to Yasukuni in 1985. [289]Safier (1997) maintained that Nakasone became the first postwar Prime Minister to declare an official visit to the Shrine in 1985. Before then, no other prime ministers visited Yasukuni, except as private persons. In response to the severe domestic and international criticism he received, Nakasone urged the government to form a commission to address the Yasukuni problem.

Shortly after Nakasone's visit, [290]China's Foreign Minister said that the visit would have "a harmful effect on the feelings of Chinese and other Asians occupied by Japan in the 1930s and

---

288   Wikipedia: Yasuhiro Nakasone. Online at http://en.wikipedia.org/wiki/Yasuhiro_Nakasone

289   Safier, Yasukuni Shrine and the Constraints on the Discourses of Nationalism in Twentieth-Century Japan. p. 41

290   Clyde Haberman, "Tokyo 40 Years Later: War Dead are Honored," The New York Times. 16 August 1985, p.2

1940s." The [291]Beijing Review called Nakasone's visit "a jarring note amid the universal calls for peace and justice," and hoped Japanese government would "bow to the historical facts and take an unequivocal stand on where the guilt and responsibility for its appalling war of aggression" lay. Nakasone's visit drew bitter criticism in China, Korea, Taiwan and quite a few South East Asian countries, not only because of Japanese atrocities committed on their lands, but also Japan's State Shinto was forced upon the citizens of these countries.

[292]Within Japan, opposition parties also vigorously attacked Nakasone, creating a huge division and stormy debates in the diet. The *Socialist Party* said the visit was "intended to coincide with a bigger military build-up. The *Socialist Party* viewed that official worship at the Shrine meant the negation of the government's duty to observe the Constitution, which prohibited government's involvement in any form of religious ceremonies. It was believed that the reason Nakasone was adamant in visiting Yasukuni was gaining the political backing of ultra-nationalist *Nihon Izokukai* (Japan Association for the Bereaved Families of the War Dead) or association of surviving families of the dead soldiers. As he visited the Shrine, his party (Liberal Democratic Party) gained more support from the association.

Nakasone had a unique political agenda among Japan's conservatives. He was well known as an advocate of constitutional revision, Japan's rearmament and the termination of Security treaty with USA. He arrived in office in 1982, "declaring that it was time to address hitherto taboo topics and settle all accounts on postwar political issues. Nakasone was very unique among Post World War II conservative politicians and experienced several conflicts with traditional conservatives.

[293]Having returned home in the fall of 1945 after fighting in the war as an Imperial Japanese Navy officer, Nakasone

---

291   Xin Jong, Nakasone's Shrine Visit Draws Fire," Beijing Review 28 (September 1985)

292   Safier, Yasukuni Shrine and the Constraints on the Discourses of Nationalism in Twentieth-Century Japan. pp. 42-45

293   Yasuhiro Nakasone. Seiji to jinsei – Nakasone Yasuhiro kaisoroku [My Life and Politics]. (Draft of translation by Nat Sayer) (Tokyo: Kodansha, 1992). pp. 5-6

witnessed firsthand the psychological and material devastation that the war brought upon Japan. In his autobiography, Nakasone stated he had the sense of humiliation and defeat as the nation's accomplishments and achievements over the two-thirds century were reduced to dust. He was deeply disappointed with Japan's former leaders who led her to defeat, and vowed to lead the nation some day to rebuild and restore Japan's strength. When Nakasone first came into politics, he was very critical of Japan's leaders who led the nation into the war, although he was consistently right wing or ultra-nationalist with no disagreement with the worldview and the interpretation of history that Yasukuni Shrine had exhibited in its Yushukan War Memorabilia Museum.[294]

[295]In 1948, Nakasone also suggested that Emperor Hirohito had to abdicate from the throne because he was at least partly responsible for the war. On January 31, 1952, he declared during questioning in the Budgetary Committee of the House of Representatives that "responsibility for having degraded the glory of modern Japan lay with Emperor Hirohito. Nakasone wanted the emperor to acknowledge "his responsibility for having driven Japan into a reckless war" by abdicating.

However, Prime Minister [296]Shigeru Yoshida (1878-1967) dismissed Nakasone's suggestion, angrily commenting that Nakasone's statement was very "non-Japanese." After more than three decades, Hirohito expressed a serious concern about Nakasone's visit to Yasukuni. Those who viewed Hirohito as a pacifist regarded Nakasone as much more nationalist than Hirohito or even Yoshida. They could argue that Nakasone wanted Hirohito to retire because he was too pacifist, not authoritarian enough and inadequate as the head of a newly resurrecting Japan. Yoshida, a traditional nationalist, believed in the emperor's literal divine nature and inviolability, so therefore was neither responsible for the inauguration of the war nor

294   Wikipedia: Yasuhiro Nakasone. Online at http://en.wikipedia.org/wiki/Yasuhiro_
        Nakasone
295   Herbert P. Bix Hirohito and the Making of Modern Japan p. 649
296   Wikipedia: Shigeru Yoshida. Online at http://en.wikipedia.org/wiki/Shigeru_
        Yoshida

the resultant defeat in it. However, being more pragmatic and utilitarian than any conservative predecessors, Nakasone believed that the emperor was useless unless he did not contribute to the national interest instead of believing in the literal meaning of the myth around him.

As an advocate of economic nationalism rather than political nationalism, Nakasone wanted Japan to use its newly created postwar economic wealth, luxury and power as the foundation of a new place for Japan in the world.

Nakasone eagerly pursued the vision to promote a new form of nationalism which was more pragmatic than the one of the previous era to transform Japan into an international state and global leader.

[297]Apart from Nakasone's ambition, *Liberal Democratic Party* (LDP), to which Nakasone belonged, had been looking for the chances to re-nationalize Yasukuni. The party embraced the Yasukuni cause vigorously due to the fact that it received support from *Nihon Izokukai* (Japan Association for the Bereaved Families of the War Dead). The LDP tried hard to press this agenda during Nakasone's leadership since at this time the party and *Nihon Izokukai* were in honeymoon. They intended to exploit the 40th anniversary of the Second World War in 1985 and the 60th anniversary of Emperor Hirohito's ascension to the throne in 1986, and so formed a commission to study the legality of official worship.

Nakasone and the LDP officials tried to use the logic that Yasukuni was not a "religious" site but a place to bereave dead soldiers or a Japanese counterpart of [298]*Arlington National Cemetery* in USA, and tried to sugarcoat an attempt to resurrect the State Shinto. In order to convince the public that Yasukuni was not a "religious" site, [299]Nakasone offered flowers purchased

---

297   Frank Baldwin. State and Religion in Japan: A Crack in the Wall?" 46
      Christianity and Crisis 154 (May 5, 1986)
298   Wikipedia: Arlington National Cemetery. Online at http://en.wikipedia.org/wiki/
      Arlington_National_Cemetery
299   Safier, Yasukuni Shrine and the Constraints on the Discourses of Nationalism in
      Twentieth-Century Japan. p. 41

with government funds and bowed only once, instead of offering sacred *sakaki* branch clapping twice, and bowing one more time as Shinto formal worship required.

[300]Nakasone also tried to convince US President Ronald Reagan, one of his close allies, and the other heads of state to pay a visit to the Yasukuni shrine. Reagan declined Nakasone's offer so he would not anger his supporters of evangelical Christian background by bowing down to what would be considered pagan gods. [301]Even Richard Nixon, who did not publicly profess Christian faith in the same way as Reagan did, responded to Christian concerns and refused to pay respects to the dead at Yasukuni as he traveled to Japan as vice president in 1953.

Nakasone's government created a committee to survey and discuss the legitimacy of the official worship by the prime minister. The commissioners to study the legality of official worship by the prime minister disagreed further as time progressed and the committee eventually fell apart. [302]Ayako Sono (曽野綾子)[303] (b. 1931), a well-known Catholic writer, and establishment intellectual, demolished Nakasone's contention that Yasukuni was not a religious site by making contradictory statements. Nakasone's logic bankrupted because Yasukuni had been a Shinto Shrine from its inception, although it had also served as a state shrine for the war dead. As Sturgeon notes, Yasukuni embraced a paradox between a religious site and a place of extreme nationalism under State Shinto. This paradox did not exist in Arlington, where faith and nationality were open to all. The commission and LDP had come to the conclusion that to make an official Shinto worship in or nationalize a shrine was

---

300   Frank Baldwin. State and Religion in Japan: A Crack in the Wall?" 46
      Christianity and Crisis 154 (May 5, 1986)
301   It was completely outrageous that US President George W. Bush, who
      professed Christian faith more loudly than Reagan in public, visited Meiji Shrine
      (another Pre-World War II Emperor Worship centre) and paid respects there as
      he traveled to Japan in the February 2002. Also, he was seriously thinking to do
      the same thing in Yasukuni, although he did not carry it out.
302   Wikipedia: Ayako Sono. Online at http://en.wikipedia.org/wiki/Ayako_Sono
303   Ayako Sono visited Yasukuni annually and publicly declared that the visit was
      not contradictory with her Christian faith at all. Her action and statement were
      total rebellion against Christ and extremely grievous in the same way as the
      visit to Meiji Shrine made by US President George W. Bush.

impossible under the current constitution as the government's own legal experts had already reached the same conclusion in 1980.

[304]As Nakasone and the LDP attempted to nationalize Yasukuni or reinstate pre-war official worship there, they met broad-based and ecumenical opposition from the religious community. The opponents included the *National Christian Council of Japan, Catholic Bishops' Council of Japan, Japan Buddhist Federation, Shinshu Federation*, and *Federation of New Religions of Japan*. These groups claim a total membership of 95 million, although many Japanese belong to more than one. Nakasone's attempt to regard Yasukuni as a place to bereave dead soldiers with a "religious" site failed, since it seemed to have required too much twist of logic and invited harsh criticisms from both opponents and traditional supporters of the Yasukuni cause.

Nakasone was once enthusiastic about re-nationalizing Yasukuni and resuscitating pre-war State Shinto using his own peculiar logic that Yasukuni was merely a memorial place for dead soldiers. But as more opposition come from both inside and outside of his country, Nakasone's enthusiasm faded and he seems to have backed off and stopped official visits to Yasukuni. In 1985, [305]Nakasone did not attend Yasukuni's *Autumn Festival*, a rite he had participated in previously as a "private person." He also skipped his New Year's visit to Yasukuni in 1986, although he had gone there for the previous two years as a private person. Instead, he held an official press conference at *Grand Ise Shrine*, showing a gesture to the right and State Shinto advocates including ultra-nationalist *Nihon Izokukai* or *Japan Association for the Bereaved Families of the War Dead*. At the end, Nakasone announced that he would not attend Yasukuni's April rites, a major event.

[306]Frank Baldwin (1986) made a concluding remark at the end of his article that Nakasone seemed to have boxed himself into a no-win situation. It seemed that the matter regarding

---

304   Baldwin. State and Religion in Japan: A Crack in the Wall?"
305   Baldwin. Ibid
306   Baldwin. Ibid

the Yasukuni Shrine and Japanese National Shinto were non-essential issues for him although there was no doubt that he supported them. Likely the main impetus for his vigorous promotion of the nationalization of Yasukuni and official Shinto worship as the prime minister of Japan in the beginning of his leadership was the support from State Shinto advocates. It is also interesting to note that having retired from politics; Nakasone was opposing Prime Minister Koizumi and Abe's official visit to Yasukuni in the beginning of the third millennium. It was likely due to the fact that he had learned a hard lesson from his failure to nationalize Yasukuni and came to the conclusion that Yasukuni was a political "black hole" and no person could expect practical benefits from it.

[307]It must be noted that during the era of Nakasone's leadership, the Rev. Masahiro Tomura, chairman of the United Church of Christ in Japan spoke on Yasukuni and the antinationalization effort" as follows:

> Yasukuni was the spiritual pillar of the emperor's
> military forces and was used to justify and glorify
> aggression. It still has that function today. Soon
> the shrine will be inspiring another generation
> of young men to die in battle for Japan and
> supporting a new militarism. To those who want
> peace, to the war dead and their relatives, this
> use of the shrine is blasphemy (Baldwin, 1986).

After Nakasone backed off and made an announcement that he would never visit the shrine as the Prime Minister of Japan, the Yasukuni controversy became dormant until Prime Minister Ryutaro Hashimoto made an official visit in 1996.

The next major controversy took place during the era of the leadership of [308]Prime Minister Ryutaro Hashimoto (橋本龍太郎) (1937–2006) in the mid nineties. [309]According to Reuters, in July 1996, Prime Minister Hashimoto visited a controversial

307   Baldwin. State and Religion in Japan: A Crack in the Wall?"
308   Wikipedia: Ryutaro Hashimoto. Online at http://en.wikipedia.org/wiki/Ryutaro_
        Hashimoto
309   Reuters, 1996

Yasukuni Shrine to the nation's war dead, including executed war criminals, breaking a decade-long taboo on Japanese leaders visiting the site. In a surprise move that risked angering victims of Japan's Second World War actions in China, the United States and other regions of the planet, Hashimoto declared the time had come for Japan to stop apologizing for honoring its war dead. "Why should it matter any more?" Hashimoto told reporters, "surely it's time to stop letting that sort of thing complicate our international relations."

Hashimoto's visit immediately brought both domestic and international disputes and protests. "We strongly protest this "official visit" by Prime Minister Hashimoto, which glorifies war and praises the war dead as "heroic spirits," said Takemitsu Ogawa, the head of a pacifist group of war victims' families. Reuters' article indicated that the visit could trouble Japan's relations with Asian neighbors at a time when it was facing criticism for refusing to provide official direct compensation to women forced into sexual slavery by Japanese troops during the war. The government wanted the victims to accept a one-time compensation through a private fund.

After Hashimoto resigned from office on 1998, no prime minister visited Yasukuni and the controversy became dormant again until Junichiro Koizume come to the office in 2001. [310]Shortly before [311]Junichiro Koizumi (小泉純一郎) (b. 1942) was elected as Prime Minister of Japan, he notified *Nihon Izokukai*, or the Japan Association for the Bereaved Families of the War Dead, that if elected Prime Minister he would make an annual visit to the Yasukuni Shrine in Tokyo on August 15, the anniversary of the end of the war.

When Koizumi made the first official visit to Yasukuni, the entire Far East region protested. Japanese ambassadors in Beijing and Seoul were summoned to ministries of foreign affairs to hear official protests. He continued, however, to visit

---

310   William Daniel Sturgeon, Japan's Yasukuni Shrine: Place of Peace or Place of Conflict? pp. 2-3
311   Wikipedia: Junichiro Koizumi. Online at http://en.wikipedia.org/wiki/Junichiro_ Koizumi

Yasukuni annually until he finally stepped down from office in September 2006. In December 2005, President Roh Moo Hyun of South Korea and Chinese Prime Minister Wen Jiabao refused an official meeting with Koizumi. Singapore and Taiwan also expressed their displeasure with Koizumi's visits. In addition, Michael Green, a former Security Council official remarked that Japan must solve this issue or risk being isolated in East Asia.

[312] William Daniel Sturgeon also maintains that Koizumi only focused on domestic political advantages and ignored the impacts on the international society that his action caused. Koizumi refused to recognize that the protests in the streets and among foreign ministries demonstrated a clear and impending danger to the relationship between Japan and her neighbors as well as the national interest and economic well being of his own country. Quoting [313]China Daily, one of China's dailies, Sturgeon noted that not only did the visits raise concerns among Japan's neighbors, or "hurt their feelings," the tensions were an unnecessary burden for the entire Far East and caused some security concerns. Koizumi resigned from office in September 2006 shortly after his last August visit to Yasukuni.

[314]Shinzo Abe (安倍晋三) (b. 1954) who took prime minister's job after Koizumi's resignation, did not make an official announcement about his future visit to Yasukuni. [315]On his official homepage he denied that Japanese troops used comfort women and dismissed Korean "revisionism" as foreign interference in Japanese domestic affairs. Abe also stated his belief that Class-A war criminals were not criminals under Japan's domestic law.

[316]In a Diet session on October 6, 2006, however, Abe had to revise his statement about comfort women and said that he accepted the report issued in 1993, written by the sitting

312   Sturgeon, Japan's Yasukuni Shrine: Place of Peace or Place of Conflict? p. 5
313   Wikipedia: China Daily. Online at http://en.wikipedia.org/wiki/China_Daily
314   Wikipedia: Shinzo Abe. Online at http://en.wikipedia.org/wiki/Shinzo_Abe#_note-1
315   Welcome to Shinzo Abe's Official Site. Online at http://newleader.s-abe.or.jp/
316   Wikipedia: Comfort women. Online at http://en.wikipedia.org/wiki/Comfort_women

cabinet secretary, Yohei Kono (河野洋平) (b. 1937), in which the Japanese government officially acknowledged the issue. [317]Abe seems to have made a significance concession to China on the shrine. Analysts suggested that he promise to refrain from high-profile visits to the shrine, although he could perhaps make personal visits without publicity. Japan's business groups have put heavy pressure on Abe to solve the Yasukuni issue, which has jeopardized growing business ties between Japan and China.

Unlike Koizumi, Abe made concessions with China partly because he had a completely different personality and political style than his predecessor. Although Abe's historical view is strongly pro-nationalist, he was more careful about the relationship with his neighbors than was Koizumi. It appears that Abe can no longer afford to follow Koizumi's reckless politics that disregarded the relationship with Japan's neighbors and caused damage to the national interest as economic groups were the most vital supporters which kept his party in power. Nevertheless, he hasn't changed his nationalist belief and agreement belief about what the Yasukuni shrine propagates. Therefore, Yasukuni critics in Japan, as well as Chinese and Korean leaders, continue to keep an eye on Abe.

Abe, Koizumi's immediate successor, did not visit the shrine in 2007 while in office. However, he did visit it on Aug. 15, 2008 and along with Koizumi on Aug. 14, 2009 on the 64th anniversary of the end of the Second World War. After Abe resigned in the Fall 2007, the nation had two LDP prime ministers. They were Yasuo Fukuda (福田康夫) (b. 1936) and Taro Aso (麻生太郎) (b. 1940) and each of them stayed in the office approximately one year. Prior to his installation as a prime minister, Fukuda announced that he would not pay respects at the Yasukuni Shrine that honors some convicted Japanese war criminals along with the country's war dead. Aso also abstained from visiting the Shrine in his terms as prime minister, seeking to smooth diplomatic relations by avoiding visits to the shrine, although he shared some of the nationalist sentiment of Yasukuni supporters.

---

317   China Institute: Japan, China reach agreement over shrine. Was available Jan. 2007: http://www.uofaweb.unalberta.ca/chinainstitute/news.cfm?story=51368

As Aso dissolved the lower house of the parliament in August 2009, a historic defeat of LDP followed and Democratic Party of Japan (DPJ) took over the power. Yukio Hatoyama (鳩山由紀夫) (b.1947) leader of the DPJ and the first DPJ prime minister, pledged not to visit a contentious shrine for Japanese war dead as part of an effort to bolster ties with China.

[318]On November 2008, Air Force Chief of Staff General Toshio Tamogami (田母神俊雄) (b.1948) of Japan's Self Defence Force (SDF) was fired for releasing a controversial article that justified the nation's aggression to her neighbours during the Second World War and denied the war-time atrocities.[319] He claimed that his country was not an aggressor in the war, but rather was tricked into involvement by the United States. Since Japan's wartime aggression remains a sensitive topic, Tamogami's article stirred an international controversy. Many of Japan's neighbours including China and South Korea were stunned by his statement. Defence Minister Yasukazu Hamada and three other senior officials were taking partial pay cuts and two bureaucrats had been reprimanded over the essay. As Japan's Defence Ministry dismissed the general, they also punished several top officials for failing to supervise the Air Force Chief. Shortly after Tamogami's dismissal, China welcomed the ministry's action.

The general had asserted that Japan was not an aggressor, Pearl Harbor was an American trap and Japan's brutal occupation of other Asian countries – which by some accounts claimed 20 million lives – wasn't that bad. Tamogami maintained that life in countries under Japanese occupation was "very moderate" compared to other colonial rulers and liberated the Asian people from oppression and improved their standard of living.

He also suggested Japan should cast off the widely held views of its Second World War culpability – and "regain its glorious history." Tamogami offered no apology, saying he believed the essay would "benefit the country and the people."

318   BBC News. Japan air force chief faces sack. October. 2008. Online at http://news.bbc.co.uk/2/hi/asia-pacific/7702374.stm
319   Wikipedia: Toshio Tamogami. Online at http://en.wikipedia.org/wiki/Toshio_Tamogami

He blatantly stated that "a country where one cannot say anything against the government's view has no democracy -- the same as North Korea." The general emphasized that his action is totally legitimate and legally protected under the freedom of speech. However, many may raise the question, "Was there more freedom of speech in pre-war Japan than North Korea?" Almost everyone would agree that if a uniformed general of the Imperial Japan spoke against the government's view, he would be executed or severely punished right away. Therefore, there is an obvious inconsistency in his action that he supports Japanese totalitarian regime or *Kokutai* prior to World-War II on one hand, but defends his action under the freedom of speech that is totally foreign to the older regime.

Monsters Returned

Going back to the story of Miyazaki's animation movie [320]*Nausicaä of the Valley of the Wind*, Nausicaä was a charismatic young princess of the peaceful *Valley of the Wind,* thousands of years after the destruction in "Seven Days of Fire," an event which destroyed human civilization and most of the earth by the God Warriors. Her name comes from the princess in the *Odyssey* who assisted *Odysseus.* Part of her character comes from a Japanese folk hero known as "the princess who loved insects," while another part was inspired by the writings of [321]Bernard Evslin (1922-1993), as he had written a more in-depth extrapolation of the character of *Odyssey*'s *Nausicaä.*

[322]Thousands of years later after the whole earth civilization was destroyed there are only small kingdoms and fiefdoms that remain along the edge of the *Sea of Corruption*, a vast forest of fungus and plants that give off poisonous gases and cover most of the Earth.

The monster God Warriors were dead for millennia and had become fossils by the time *Nausicaä* was born. Nevertheless, one inactivated God Warrior fetus was lying for thousands of

---

320   Wikipedia: Nausicaä of the Valley of the Wind (film). Online at http://en.wikipedia.org/wiki/Nausica%C3%A4_of_the_Valley_of_the_Wind_(film)
321   Wikipedia: Bernard Evslin. Online at http://en.wikipedia.org/wiki/Bernard_Evslin
322   Hayao Miyazaki Web, 2006. Online at http://www.nausicaa.net/miyazaki/

years underneath *Valley of the Wind. Princess Kushana,* who led *Torumekians Force* that occupied the Valley, pursued the fetus of the God Warrior vigorously and finally discovered it. Then she attempted to activate and use him to destroy the sea of corruption which tormented humanity for thousands of years, along with her human enemies. Kushana almost completed her mission to activate the ancient monster who almost destroyed humanity.

A massive humanoid form appeared, and the newly created God Warrior beamed pure energy at a huge group of *Ohmu* or gigantic insects that tormented humanity, at Kushana's command. But the God Warrior was birthed much too soon and the body started to pour from its inner skeletal structure. When the second nuclear beam was emitted and another large group of Ohmu was destroyed, the nuclear core of the God Warrior was exhausted and he crumbled into a pile of liquid flesh and bones.

The attempt of Koizumi and other Japanese conservatives to revive the Shinto cult from the bottom of Hades was as foolish as Kushana's attempt to revive the prehistoric monster. Once activated and fully mature, the God Warrior would stop taking orders from any human beings including Kushana herself. She was fortunate that the monster was not complete yet when she woke him up, so that he crumbled into a pile of liquid flesh and bones. Otherwise, the monster would be out of control and destroy everything including *Torumekians Force* and Kushana herself. The God Warrior was bred and programmed only to kill and destroy. It was why handful of God Warriors terminated humanity and its civilization in only seven days. Likewise, once the Yasukuni nationalist cult gains more popularity among Japanese public, it will be beyond a political leader's control.

[323]Harry Harootunia (1999) maintains that reinstating the link between state or the old imperial bureaucracy and the

---

323   Harry Harootunian. Memory, Mourning, and National Morality: Yasukuni Shrine and the Reunion of State and Religion in Postwar Japan. In Peter Vander Veer & Hartmut Lehmann, eds. (Princeton, NJ: Princeton University Press, 1999) p. 147

Yasukuni Shrine, devoted to preserving the spirit of Japan's war dead by any form, means returning her to a time people were socialized into performing unhesitant service to the emperor. He also expresses concern that conservatives campaigned against apologies made by Japan's past prime ministers made about wartime atrocities in China and Korea. Harootunia stated that:

> The very people who campaigned loudest against an apology are the same people who have promoted the move to persuade the state to assume responsibility for managing the Yasukuni Shrine, to reconcile polity and religion as it was envisaged by the Meiji state in the ninety century (Harootunia, 1999).

Japan's ultra-nationalists and followers of the Yasukuni cult campaigned loudly against apologies made for the past by the leaders with a moderate stance and for the reunification of state and Shinto. These fanatics made bold attempts to justify Japan's military aggression to her neighbors in East Asia, rewrite the history and resuscitate pre-Second World War monsters, which created woes and troubles in Japan and her neighboring nations. The new nationalism could be compared to an unborn fetus of a God Warrior that Kushana recovered from the underground of the *Valley of the Wind* in Miyazaki's movie. By this comparison, it would be an extremely foolish attempt to wake up an unborn fetus of one of the monsters created by the leaders of Meiji government buried underneath Yasukuni Shrine's. It would be self evident that the moment to activate the monster would be a complete disaster as in the moment of opening [324]*Pandora's Box* in the Greek mythology.

In the story of [325]*Mighty Morphin Power Rangers*[326] (1993-1996), an American live-action television series, [327]*Rita Repulsa,* a witch and evil queen is mistakenly freed from the

---

324   Wikipedia: Pandora. Online at http://en.wikipedia.org/wiki/Pandora's_Box
325   Power Rangers Universe. Online at http://www.geocities.com/Hollywood/ Lot/6151/NewMainPage.htm
326   Wikipedia: Power Rangers. Online at http://en.wikipedia.org/wiki/Power_ Rangers
327   Wikipedia: Rita Repulsa. Online at http://en.wikipedia.org/wiki/Rita_Repulsa

dumpster prison on the Moon by careless astronauts after a long imprisonment following defeat by a wise old sage named *Zordon*. The astronauts discovered the extra-terrestrial container and inadvertently released Rita and her followers from 10,000 years of confinement. Upon her release, Rita and her army of evil goblins and monsters set their sights on conquering the earth, the nearest planet. She possessed a wand that could be used to transform her monsters to gigantic sizes and torture the Power Rangers.

Mighty Morphin Power Rangers was a recreation of a Japanese tokusatsu television series [328]*Kyouryuu Sentai Zyuranger* (恐竜戦隊ジュウレンジャー) (1992-1993) from which the footage was extensively used. Rita's original character in the Japanese series was named *Bandora* and sealed away by the *Mysterious Hermit Barza* (不思議仙人バーザ *Fushigi Sennin Bāza*), a counterpart of Zordon in the ancient days before the humanity was created. The name Bandora seemed to have a linkage with the idea of Pandora's Box. A total disaster started as the astronauts open the urn in which the evil queen and monsters are sealed. Once it was unsealed the process was totally irreversible. Likewise, once Japan's ultra-nationalists that follow the order of Rita, like Queen Amaterasu, released from the box, they would be totally out of control and even the government could not do anything with them.

---

328   Wikipedia: Kyouryuu Sentai Zyuranger. Online at http://en.wikipedia.org/wiki/
Kyouryuu_Sentai_Zyuranger

[329]Princess Kushana activates God Warrior. Hayao Miyazaki. Nausicaä of the Valley of the Wind, 1984.[330]

---

329   Was available June 2010; http://darknarice3.hp.infoseek.co.jp/
      SS_2007_12/20071217_00.jpg
330   The picture is used under "fair dealing" (Canada) and "fair use" (USA)
      provisions in copyright law.

CHAPTER 9

KOKUTAI, STATE SHINTO & EMPEROR'S ROLE

For Japan's leaders before the Second World War, there was nothing more important than the continuation of the monarchy or the emperor system and *Kokutai,* or a spiritual community centered on the emperor. By the summer of 1945, Imperial Japan had lost almost all the Combined Fleet of the Imperial Navy, war ships and aircraft carriers and many crucial military factories were utterly destroyed by bombing. Because these factories were destroyed, Japan had lost her industrious stamina to recover the loss by reproducing military products to fight back the Allied Force. In addition, Germany and Italy, two important allies of Imperial Japan, had already surrendered. The armor of the entire nation ripped it nearly naked in the summer of 1945.

Potsdam Declaration & Surrender

So the continuation of the war was increasingly difficult, and chances of winning almost completely annihilated. Leaders of Imperial Japan had virtually no choice than to accept an unconditional surrender to the Allied Force. Former Prime Minister Prince Fumimaro Konoe suggested Japan's surrender to the Allied Forces on the condition that the emperor system was sustained. The Allied Force issued *Potsdam Declaration* on July 26, 1945 as a Japanese surrender. It outlined the terms of surrender for Japan by Harry S Truman, Winston Churchill, and Chiang Kai-Shek, as agreed upon at the Potsdam Conference. [331]The content of the declaration included:

---

331   Wikipedia: Potsdam Declaration. Online at http://en.wikipedia.org/wiki/ Potsdam_Declaration

- Militarism in Japan must end.
- Japan would be occupied until the basic objectives set out in this proclamation were met.
- The terms of the Cairo Declaration would be carried out and Japanese sovereignty would be limited to the islands of Honshu, Hokkaido, Kyushu, Shikoku and such minor islands as the Allies determined.
- The Japanese army would be completely disarmed and allowed to return home.
- Those who had led Japan to war must be permanently and finally discredited, and abandoned.
- War criminals would be punished including those who had "visited cruelties upon our prisoners." Freedom of speech, of religion, and of thought, as well as respect for fundamental human rights would be established.
- Japan should be permitted to maintain a viable industrial economy but not industries that would enable her to re-arm for war.
- The treaty was not intended to enslave Japanese as a race or as a nation.
- Allied forces would be withdrawn from Japan as soon as these objectives had been accomplished.
- The statement - "We call upon the government of Japan to proclaim now the unconditional surrender of all Japanese armed forces, and to provide proper and adequate assurances of their good faith in such action. The alternative for Japan is prompt and utter destruction."

Konoe strongly suggested to the emperor to accept it as soon as possible because of the statement "prompt and utter destruction" as the alternative. He believed the emperor and the nation's leadership could no longer afford to delay the decision-making.

Mystery of Delayed Surrender

[332]Unable to decide to end the war unless the future of the throne and the all important prerogatives of its occupant were absolutely guaranteed, Prime Minister [333]Kantaro Suzuki (1867-1948), his cabinet and the *Supreme War Leadership Council* could not be brought to frame a peace maneuver until after two atomic bombs had been dropped.

[334]Joseph Kitagawa (1990) remarks how leaders struggled for the maintenance of Kokutai in the last and devastating phase of the war. Kitagawa contends that:

> It sounds astonishing, but it is true, that even at the end of a devastating Pacific war, the leaders of Japanese militarism expected to continue to rule the people, preserving the previous system and defending the national polity including the imperial system and the State Shinto, etc. (Kitagawa, 1990)

It is nearly unbelievable that in such an extraordinary desperate circumstance, the continuation of Kokutai and the emperor system was still the most crucial issue that Japanese leaders could not be comprise. After the atomic bombs were dropped, however, Japan had no choice but to finally accept an unconditional surrender to the Allied Forces. There was a secret discussion between leaders of Japan and Allied Forces regarding the survival of the emperor system. There didn't seem to be any room of discussion or negotiation as Japan had lost almost everything by the time of surrender. But after the war ended, the Allied Forces allowed retention of the emperor system as Konoe had hoped because Gen. MacArthur viewed the emperor system as a useful tool to control the Japanese public.

---

332   Herbert P. Bix. Hirohito and the Making of Modern Japan p. 498
333   Wikipedia: Kantaro Suzuki. Online at http://en.wikipedia.org/wiki/Kantaro_ Suzuki
334   Joseph Kitagawa. Some Reflections and Its Relationship to the Imperial System. Journal of Religious Studies, 1990 p. 167

[335]Also, on the American side, many viewed the emperor as a pacifist and helpless figurehead. [336]Joseph Grew (1880-1965) a conservative Republican regarded Emperor Hirohito as a person who held the key to Japan's surrender. According to him, Hirohito was a constitutionalist and a pacifist, but unfortunately had been a "puppet" of the militarists for more than a decade prior to the war. Bix notes that Grew had the power to influence the American public although he knew nothing or little about the "Japanese body politic" or politics around the emperor system.

Grew was also known for his *queen bee analogy* - that if you killed the queen bee, the emperor, all Japanese would die. His analogy seemed absurd and irrational. But during the Second World War, it did seem as if almost all Japanese soldiers and civilians were brainwashed so that they were ready to die for the emperor anytime. As an analogy, to attempt to dismantle a bomb before removing certain wires will cause a fatal explosion. It seems, therefore, that Grew's insights, that killing the emperor would activate a pre-programmed self-destructive sequence and destroy everything, were correct. He failed, however, to understand the complexity and complication of the [337]extremely complex Japanese court culture and politics around the emperor.

[338]President Harry Truman (1884 -1972) and secretary of State [339]James Byrnes (1879 – 1972) rejected [340]Grew's efforts to include a clause guaranteeing the retention of the imperial house in the draft of Potsdam Declaration. But his ability to influence the public through charm and charisma turned the public in his favour. Although the president initially rejected

335   Herbert P. Bix Hirohito and the Making of Modern Japan p. 478
336   Wikipedia: Joseph Grew. Online at http://en.wikipedia.org/wiki/Joseph_Grew
337   Generally speaking Japanese and other East Asian societies were considered higher context than the West. Japanese court-culture was extremely higher-context and decoding the communications there was quite difficult even for average Japanese.
338   Wikipedia: Harry S. Truman. Online at http://en.wikipedia.org/wiki/Harry_S._Truman
339   Wikipedia: James F. Byrnes. Online at http://en.wikipedia.org/wiki/James_Byrnes
340   Joseph C Grew. Turbulent Era: A Diplomatic Record of Forty Years, 1904-1945, vol 2 (Boston: Houghton Mufflin, Co., 1992), p. 1435

Grew's proposal, Grew eventually influenced the American public to persuade Washington's decision to retain Hirohito's throne.

[341]Bix, quoting a diary of [342]Koichi Kido (木戸幸一) (1889 –1977), the Lord Keeper of the Privy Seal, stated that twice on both July 25 and 31, Hirohito made clear to Kido that the imperial *regalia* had to be defended "at all cost." Bix understands this as evidence of Hirohito's obsession with the survival of imperial house. There is no doubt that there was nothing more important to him than the *regalia* or the continuation of the imperial line. Retention of the line was Hirohito's sole responsibility to his Kami and he felt he had no responsibility to the citizens of Japan or any living human beings above that.[343]

There remain questions about Bix's interpretation of Hirohito's statement in Kido's diary, however, as Kido seemed to write it to protect the emperor from criminal prosecution. If Hirohito had told him the same thing simply because he was obsessed with the survival of the monarchy, Kido would not have recorded it. It seems safe to assume that Kido was wise enough to know Hirohito's defending of the regalia to meet responsibility to Kami, instead of Japan's citizens, would seem outrageous to the GHQ officials, average Americans or any non-Japanese.

Therefore, what Hirohito likely meant was unless the future of the monarchy was guaranteed, ultranationalists in the military would not agree with the surrender. Otherwise, Kido would not have recorded his statement for the protection of his master from criminal prosecution. If Hirohito had stated that they must defend the emperor's regalia with cost to all citizens of Japan, Kido would have chosen to delete this from the diary because it would guarantee his immediate guilty verdict and execution.

Kido maintained that from the beginning to the end of the war, the emperor and Kido himself were staunchly against the war and ultra-nationalism in the military. Critics note that Kido's diary somehow overstated the military leaders' guilt and

---

341   Herbert P. Bix Hirohito and the Making of Modern Japan p. 502
342   Koichi Kido. Kido Koichi Nikki, ge. [Diary of Koichi Kido]. (Tokyo: Tokyo University Press, 1966)
343   Wikipedia: Kōichi Kido. Online at http://en.wikipedia.org/wiki/Koichi_Kido

responsibility for the war to prove the innocence of the emperor and himself. Military leaders who were sentenced to death were furious as Kido's diary was released to the court and they cursed Kido in the last moments before execution. His testimony, however, was not good enough to prove his innocence or that of the emperor, so Kido was found guilty and sentenced to life imprisonment. He spent time in Sugamo Prison in Tokyo until he was released from prison in 1953 due to health problems. Nevertheless, Kido was pleased that Emperor Hirohito was exemplified from criminal prosecution.

MacArthur Saved Hirohito & Emperor System

When the war was over, Emperor Hirohito, therefore, was rescued from the hands of executioners by Gen. MacArthur and remained on the throne after the war. Athough there is no written record, the authority of the Allied Forces likely reconstructed Hirohito's personal history. They had to rewrite his entire wartime record to "prove" his innocence. Washington and Gen. MacArthur rescued him, not because he was innocent, but because he was useful for the Occupation Force to control Japan's post Second World War public. They feared that Japan as a nation might fall apart or become totally chaotic similar to today's Iraq if they tried and punished Hirohito as a war criminal.

The ground to defend Hirohito's innocence was the Meiji Constitution, in which the emperor was reigning, but did not possess *de facto* ruling power. While Hirohito was venerated as "the son of the heaven," an all-powerful embodiment of the unity of Shinto and the State, he was in fact constitutionally constrained. The ground in the Meiji Constitution would provide enough evidence that Hirohito was in the position to reign, but not control the nation, so he was not as guilty as Hitler and Mussolini or even Tojo in terms of crimes against peace or humanity.

But being constitutionally constrained did not mean being completely powerless or having no responsibility at all. It is difficult to find evidence to prove that he was [344]a "prisoner and

---

344   Hidenari Terasaki & Mariko Terasaki Miller, eds., Showa Tenno Dokuhakuroku

powerless puppet of the militarists" who was not involved in the war at all. It is fair to say that although he was not a dictator who controlled the entire nation, he had at least some responsibility for the commencement of the war and all other atrocities that Japan had committed during the war.

Though he was not a cold-blooded, ruthless despot like Hitler and Saddam Hussein, his innocent and harmless image did not likely represent the real historical Hirohito. This was a fictitious image created by the Japanese establishment after Gen. MacArthur covered up the darkest part of his personal history. It was not difficult to save his life from execution and give him a prison sentence as he did not possess a *de facto* ruling power. It did, however, require highly skilful, clever and elaborate collaboration between Gen. MacArthur and the Japanese ruling class to secure Hirohito's public image and throne.

As mentioned previously, Hirohito quoted an ancient [345]Chinese Proverb "If you don't go into the cave of the tiger, how are you going to get its cub?" and viewed Tojo as a competent, diligent, sincere and loyal "tiger cub." He made a conscious decision to own an exotic pet, and his most loyal pet destroyed the entire nation. So therefore Gen. MacArthur and the International Tribunal gave an irresponsible pet owner clemency by saying that "It's not him but his cat which killed thousands of Japanese, American and Chinese soldiers and civilians in all over East Asia."

[346]Joseph Kitagawa (1990) noted that the Allied Powers decided to maintain the "imperial system" due to the insistence of Washington to use the imperial institution to expedite a smooth transition from prewar to postwar conditions in Japan under the Occupation Forces. For many people in Japan the simple fact that the imperial institution was kept, for whatever reasons, meant continuity with traditional Japan. They found it very comforting to learn that the Occupation Forces would

[Monologue of Showa Emperor]. (Tokyo: Bunshun Bunko, 1995)

345   Simran Khurana. Top 10 Chinese Proverbs. Online at http://quotations.about.com/cs/chineseproverbs/tp/10_chinese.htm

346   Joseph Kitagawa. Some Reflections and Its Relationship to the Imperial System. Journal of Religious Studies, 1990 p. 167

keep the imperial institution, even if the throne had a different meaning to the foreign rulers. Such a sentiment was shared by a large number of conservatives and rural people, and by members of families that had lost sons during the war, all of whom had felt comfortable in the prewar world of State Shinto and deified emperors. To them postwar Japan was not qualitatively different from prewar Japan, except for the fact that Japan had gambled and lost the war.

Kitagawa observed that this was the case because the imperial institution was completely fused with their daily living and belief system. Kitagawa's view states:

> [347]At least the Occupation Forces and Washington realized that the imperial institution was a harmless, ancient mummy, but that, if preserved in its modernized form, it might again be manipulated by narcissistic, ultraconservative politicians. Hence the American pressure on the Japanese government to have the Emperor proclaim on New Year's Day, 1946, his now famous declaration of humanity, rejecting the myth-shrouded notion of a deified imperial system as a fanciful notion (Kitagawa, 1990).

Gen. MacArthur and Occupation Forces tried to neutralize the emperor system by Hirohito's declaration of humanity as a way to attempt to eliminate the danger of resuscitating Second World War Emperor Cult.

Ohma the Good God Warrior

Going back once more to Miyazaki's Nausicaä's story, Princess Kushana of the Torumekians force activated a leftover *God Warrior*, or one of prehistoric monsters. But he did not last more than few minutes because of the premature activation. Miyazaki wrote a [348]comic version of Nausicaä with quite a

347   Joseph Kitagawa. Some Reflections and Its Relationship to the Imperial
       System. Journal of Religious Studies, 1990 p. 167
348   Nausicaa Glossary - Full with Pictures. Online at http://nausicaa.wanfear.com/
       Manga/Glossary/Full/original.htm

different story.[349] In the comic version, Nausicaä instead of Kushana activated the God Warrior. Unlike Kushana's God Warrior he took enough time for the activation and therefore survived. He had as much power as Kushana's God Warrior, but he was good and had a human personality. Nausicaä named him *Ohma* and used his power to save the world. Once he was named, Ohma immediately developed a strong intellect, referring to himself as an arbiter of justice. Ohma regarded Nausicaä as his mother and obeyed whatever orders she gave him. At the end of the story, Ohma died while defeating his enemies to obey Nausicaä' s order in the final battle of the story.

Gen. MacArthur's attempt to keep Hirohito on the throne and use him for the democratization of Japan somehow resembled Nausicaä's attempt to raise Ohma to be a good warrior. In fact Hirohito did everything Gen. MacArthur wanted like Ohma the good God Warrior in the comic version of Nausicaä. This action was based on the philosophy that even the most destructive monster could be used for good purposes. It seemed to have worked well for a while at least during the time Gen. MacArthur was in Japan. However, did it produce any negative effects in the long-term?

Hirohito's Exoneration & Negative Impacts

[350]Kiyohiko Ikeda (2003) contends that Gen. MacArthur made a decision to give Hirohito immunity from any criminal prosecutions based on his "noble character." There was no precedent either in Japan or the United States that criminal charges were pressed or not pressed against someone based on that individual's character. [351]Gen. MacArthur not only exonerated Hirohito but in doing so ignored the advice of many members of the imperial family and Japanese intellectuals who publicly asked for the abdication of the Emperor and the implementation of regency. In fact Prince Mikasa, Hirohito's

---

349   Wikipedia: Nausicaä of the Valley of the Wind (manga). Online at http://en.wikipedia.org/wiki/Nausica%C3%A4_of_the_Valley_of_the_Wind_(manga)
350   Ikeda, Kiyohiko, et al. Tenno no senso sekinin saiko [Reconsider emperor's war responsibility]. (Tokyo: Yosensha Bunko, 2003)
351   Wikipedia: Douglas MacArthur. Online at http://en.wikipedia.org/wiki/Douglas_MacArthur

youngest brother, stood up in a meeting of the private council in February 1946 and urged his brother to take responsibility for the defeat. Gen. MacArthur's decision, therefore, seems subjective, erratic and possibly somewhat outrageous as it was not supported by any objective or even circumstantial evidences to validate the emperor's innocence.

According to Kiyohiko Ikeda, this decision produced serious and detrimental effects to the culture since a person with the most responsible position did not take responsibility. Ikeda states that the exoneration of the emperor had a negative impact to the Japanese Post Second World War society by producing a "culture of irresponsibility." He maintains that Japanese politicians and high ranking government bureaucrats accused of various crimes such as sex scandals, embezzlement or fraud have often been exemplified from criminal charges or acquitted partly because of this "culture of irresponsibility" that Gen. MacArthur created when he rescued Hirohito.

[352]Joseph Kitagawa, who used the analogy of ancient mummy for the emperor system, also contends that if it was preserved in its modernized or toxic way, narcissistic ultranationalist politicians might again manipulate it. The ancient mummy who apparently looked harmless could once again be transformed into a powerful, gigantic, and destructive artificial life form like Frankenstein's monster. Some view what was done did sufficiently seal the monster for good. Nausicaä's Ohma, in the comic version, died when finally defeated by his enemies, eliminating any chances to be used by evil people in future were eliminated. In the same way as Nausicaä utilized Ohma the God Warrior, Gen. MacArthur used the power of the emperor system to bring about Japan's democratization smoothly and peacefully. Ulike Ohma, however, Japan's emperor system did not die when Gen. MacArthur left Japan. Both MacArthur and Hirohito were long dead by 2000, but the emperor system continues to exist. Neither would likely be able to predict the long-term effects what now seems to be irresponsible action.

---

352   Joseph Kitagawa. Some Reflections and Its Relationship to the Imperial System. Journal of Religious Studies, 1990 p. 167

Danger of Waking up Evil Monsters

[353]Harry Harootunia (1999) expressed the following concern about retention of Hirohito on the throne in his writing that:

> At the heart of this repetition is the imperial house
> and its god-man emperor, who is descended
> from Amaterasu, the Sun Goddess. Instead of
> executing the emperor as a war criminal, the US.
> Occupation resuscitated and transformed him
> into the figure of bourgeois family man no longer
> divine. But this role was simply superimposed
> on the older figure like a palimpsest that allowed
> older association of divinity and authority to
> filter through the overlay (Harootunia, 1999).

Harootunia contends that Gen. MacArthur and US occupation forces made pre-Second World War monsters dormant by depriving the emperor's divinity only instead of his throne. So the Emperor Cult, *Kokutai* and State Shinto etc. were simply sealed instead of destroyed or annihilated. Harootunia sees the danger of the retention of the emperor system and how keeping the former divine-man on the throne might cause further complications down the road. The temporary dormant monster would wake up and look for food sooner or later. Likewise, in another metaphor, unless the cancer cells are totally eradicated from the body, they can come back sooner or later. Regarding the danger of resuscitating old *Kokutai* based nationalism, Harootunia states:

> If, moreover, the imperial line was
> emblematic of Japan's uniqueness, it also
> guaranteed claims of ethnic homogeneity
> and social cohesion (Harootunia, 1999).

In other words, retention of the imperial line brings out the concept of the uniqueness and superiority of Japanese ethnicity.

---

353   Harry Harootunian. Memory, Mourning, and National Morality: Yasukuni
      Shrine and the Reunion of State and Religion in Postwar Japan. In Peter
      Vander Veer & Hartmut Lehmann, eds. (Princeton, NJ: Princeton University
      Press, 1999) p. 147

The emphasis on the maintenance of ethnic homogeneity comes from worst kind of nationalism - almost comparable to Nazi Germany and its form of criminal activity. This ethnocentrism can bring about forms of *hate crimes* by today's standards.

Counter-productive Anachronisms

Surprisingly, many politicians and other influential people in the Japanese establishment had the view that "end of Japan was the end of the world," and were not able to think beyond the border of their nation. [354]Takatoku Nakajo (2002) who was CEO of *Asahi Breweries*, one of Japan's major beer companies, wrote that the real danger of the borderless world was a stream of globalization, which might annihilate ethnicities and ethnic cultures. He viewed that people without proper ethnicity were *nenashigusa* (根無し草) that meant "rootless grass" or creatures without souls. For Nakajo, the survival of Japan as a nation-state and the retention of the national identity were most essential and the emperor system was *raison d'etre* or the pivotal factor for everyone in the country and there was nothing more important than that. His mind was not programmed to think about the world after all state-nations cease to exist. I believe that those individuals whose spiritual roots belonged to earthly matters like nation-states or ethnicities are extremely pitiful and miserable.

Short-sighted people who are not able to see the world beyond their own horizon, including ultranationalists in Japan, can be thought to resemble holographic people in the *StarTrek* Universe. They are similar to artificial, computer-generated life forms who are fully functional as long as they are within the range of a *holo-projector*. Once they go beyond a certain distance from the projector, however, they disappear or are annihilated. For the ultra-nationalists, Japan as a nation-state was a vital *holo-projector* and the emperor system was essential to keep that projector running. They were life forms not programmed to think about anything beyond the nation-state to which they belonged. They still live in the pre-war concept of the *Kokutai* or "spiritual

---

354   Takatoku Nakajo. Ojiichan, Senso no Koto o Oshiete [Grandpa, teach me about the war]. (Tokyo: Shogakkan Bunko, 2002)

Community" of the Japanese nation of which the emperor was the head.

Nakajo was also known as one of key members of [355]*Keidanren Federation of Economic Organizations* in Japan. While the association was reluctant to agree with Koizumi's Visit to Yasukuni, Nakajo was a fervent supporter of Koizumi's visits and Yasukuni's cause. Most members in the Keidanren were afraid of losing sales in China and Korea by offending Japan's neighbours. It is a good thing that he is not current CEO because if he were running the company, *Asahi Breweries* would likely lose sales instantaneously in China and Korea and soon be out of business. Business owners and CEO in the era of globalization must have global perspectives and stay away from a narrow nationalistic ideology.

[356]Karl Marx (1818 – 1883) was correct in maintaining that nation-states would dissolve at the end of the modern era in [357]his book "the Capital." He also maintained that no workers have nationalities or citizenship of any nation-state. It was the same concept that Christians were [358]sojourners and ultimately belong to God's nation. I would add that in the era of globalization, no capitalists or business owners have a nationality or can afford to have citizenship in any nation-state. For business owners and CEOs today, leaving any form of obsolete nationalism and ethnocentrism behind and dedicating themselves to the globalist worldview is mandatory for survival.

They have to follow the supreme principles, "Customers are always right." To a CEO who can't follow these principles, [359]Donald Trump would say, "You are fired." In the era of global capitalism, any kind of nationalism is antithetical to the supreme business principles or the [360]*Rules of Acquisition*. Nakajo and

355   Encyclopædia Britannica: Keidanren. Online at http://www.britannica.com/eb/
      article-9044983/Keidanren
356   Wikipedia: Karl Marx. Online at http://en.wikipedia.org/wiki/Karl_Marx
357   Karl Marx, Capital: A Critique of Political Economy. (London, UK: Penguin
      Classics, 1867/1992)
358   First Peters 1:17
359   Wikipedia: Donald Trump. Online at http://en.wikipedia.org/wiki/Donald_Trump
360   Wikipedia: Rules of Acquisition. Online at http://en.wikipedia.org/wiki/Rules_of_
      Acquisition

any other Yasukuni supporters within Keidanren Federation of Economic Organizations could soon be relics.

In early 2010, when Toyota experienced a downfall because of manufacturing errors and the resultant legal conflicts in the USA, LDP leaders as the opposition lawmakers made seemingly anachronistic comments. They said, "If we were Japan's government, we would support Toyota and intervene with US government and consumers". This is based on the assumption that Toyota is a strictly "Japanese" company that belongs to Japan. However, there is a reality that the company is a global corporation and not Japanese anymore. If it still belongs to Japan, it also belongs to the United States, Canada, China or other industrious nations.

Yakuza Uyoku & Vampires without Souls

Ultra-nationalist groups who followed the Yasukuni Cult attempted to resuscitate the emperor-centred *Kokutai* are still active, often act as terrorist groups. Some of these ultra-nationalist called Ninkyo Uyoku (任侠右翼) or Yakuza Uyoku who belong to Yakuza (Japanese gangs) groups. They are extremely dangerous and highly professional killers.

[361]*The Devil of Nangking* (2006) by [362]Mo Hayder, a popular novel and one of best sellers of 2006, is based on the story of the wartime atrocity that Japanese soldiers committed in China. It tells the story of *Grey*, a young female sociology major from the UK who visits *Shi Chongming,* an elderly visiting professor of the University of Tokyo from China. She seeks information about atrocities committed by Japanese soldiers during the 1937 invasion of Nanking. As a child, the professor had a horrendous experience of abuse by Japanese soldiers, but he refused to help the student. Instead, he gave her a warning how powerful and dangerous the "right wings" in Japan are saying:

> Do you know how powerful the right wing is
> in Japan? Do you know the people who have
> been attacked for talking about it? MacArthur

---

361   Mo Hayder. The Devil of Nangking. (London, UK: Penguin Books, 2006)
362   Wikipedia: Mo Hayder. Online at http://en.wikipedia.org/wiki/Mo_Hayder

> ensured that the right wing are the fear-
> mongers they are today. It is quite simple.
> We do not talk about it (Hayder, 2006).

"Right wings" or *uyoku* in Japan are not simply political conservatives, but extreme and fanatic ultra-nationalist groups who dare to practice terrorist activities. They also have a strong linkage with Yakuza or Japanese gangsters that create a great fear among the Japanese. Their funds come mainly from drug trafficking and other illegal activities. The average Japanese fears *uyoku* or "right wing" ultra-nationalist political activists a great deal because they are also Yakuza and terrorist groups disturbing their peaceful life.

So when the Nanking survivor refuses to help Grey with her novel, she drifts into a well-paying job as a nightclub hostess. Then she meets a mysterious customer named *Fuyuki*, an elderly Yakuza *Oyabun* or gangster boss who happens to have been a perpetrator in a Nanking massacre when he was a young soldier of Imperial Japan. As soon as Shi Chongming learns that Grey had contact with Fuyuki, he promises to provide her the information she wanted in exchange for the knowledge about a secret elixir that sustained Fuyuki. So the British student and old Chinese professor work side by side to spy on the elderly Yakuza Oyabun. Mo Hayder describes Fuyuki as a Yakuza leader and ultra-nationalist activist who possesses his own secret army. In fact, the author describes Fuyuki as a typical *Yakuza Uyoku* who is an ultra-nationalist political activist and gangster at the same time, so greatly feared by Japan's general public.

[363]In August 2006, an extreme ultranationalist *Yakuza Uyoku* like Fuyuki in Hayder's novel torched and burned down the parental home of Koichi Kato, a veteran lawmaker and onetime prime ministerial candidate who was critical of Prime Minister Koizumi's visit to Yasukuni. In April 17, 2007, [364]*Iccho Ito*, the

---

363   Steven Clemons. The Rise of Japan's Thought Police. The Washington Post Company. August. 2006. Online at http://www.washingtonpost.com/wp-dyn/content/article/2006/08/25/AR2006082501176.html?nav=rss_print/outlook

364   Hiroshi Hiyama. Nagasaki mayor dies after shooting. Yahoo News. April. 2007. Online at http://news.yahoo.com

mayor of Nagasaki died after being shot by a man who police said was a member of a gang with links to Yamaguchigumi, the country's largest crime syndicate. Police said that Ito's killer was motivated by a personal grudge against the mayor rather than right wing ideology. They did not find a clear answer as to whether the perpetrator was politically motivated by *Yakuza Uyoku* or simply Yakuza. Ito was an outspoken pacifist who was born one month after the best-known event in Nagasaki's history - the world's second and last atomic bombing on August 9, 1945 that killed more than 70,000 people. Nagasaki had another attack on its mayor by *Yakuza Uyoku*. In January 1990, a right wing extremist shot and wounded the then mayor Hitoshi Motoshima for saying he believed the late Emperor Hirohito bore responsibility for the Second World War. Fortunately, Motoshima survived.

Post-war Japan had a history of right wing terrorism accompanying assassination of politicians who were liberal, socialist and moderately conservative or right wing in the western sense. The last political assassination prior to Ito was in October 2002, when a rightist stabbed to death an opposition lawmaker campaigning to expose corruption, Koki Ishii, outside his Tokyo home with a 30-centimetre (12-inch) blade. Also, in October 12, 1969, a right-wing terrorist stabbed to death [365]Inejiro Asanuma (1898-1960), also an opposition lawmaker, and head of the *Japanese Socialist Party*. He was famous for speaking publicly about socialism and economic and cultural reforms, something that angered the right wing.

As Mo Hayder's Shi Chongming stated, Yakuza Uyoku and any other extreme ultra-nationalist groups are powerful and dangerous and might attack anyone who does not support their political agenda. Because of this, missionaries and Christian workers in Japan need to exercise extra caution. As Jesus said in the Bible, "You must be as [366]*shrewd as serpents*" when dealing with these groups, while still expressing Christian love. They are

---

365   Wikipedia: Inejiro Asanuma. Online at http://en.wikipedia.org/wiki/Inejiro_
       Asanuma
366   Matthew 10:16

diabolic, ruthless and antisocial groups of people who intend to resuscitate Japan's national Shinto and Kokutai, the Siamese twins of dangerous terrorist institutions based on a slanted view on the history.

In a sense, the Yakuza Uyoku members resembled "vampires without souls" in [367]*Buffy the Vampire Slayer* (1997-2003), a two time Emmy-winning and Golden Globe nominated American cult television series. Vampires are formerly human beings with flesh and blood, but who abandon the human soul as they became vampires and transformed into creatures that simply follow the instinct programmed by the devil to kill, steal and destroy. [368]Jeffrey L. Pasley (2003) maintains that to separate a human being from his or her soul liberates he or she from the moral qualms and sentimental feelings that impede the ability to compete and dominate. Vampires without souls are cyborg soldiers who are reprogrammed by the devil to perform evil acts as the conscience and sentiment that ordinary humans possess have been deleted from their minds.

Likewise, Yakuza Uyoku soldiers are cyborgs reprogrammed by their *Oyabuns* or bosses. In [369]Yakuza society, when someone joins a group or *kumi*, this person must go through a rite of drinking a cup of sake offered by the Oyabun and become his Kobun or foster child following the *code of jingi* (仁義) or justice and duty. The oyabun-kobun relationship is formalized by the ceremonial sharing of sake from a single cup.

This ritual also indicates that the individual abandons his free will and becomes a slave or personal property of Oyabun. He must obey Oyabun's order no matter how unethical or unreasonable it is, since he gave his soul to the Oyabun. Yakuza Uyoku are as dangerous as Buffy's vampires and they terrorize Japanese society because their souls are properties of Oyabuns who gives them orders. If the Oyabun decides that some politician must be eliminated because he or she has committed

---

367   Wikipedia: Buffy the Vampire Slayer. Online at http://en.wikipedia.org/wiki/
      Buffy_the_Vampire_Slayer
368   James, B. South, Pasley, Jeffrey L. et al. Buffy the Vampire Slayer and
      Philosophy (London, UK: Open Court Publishing Company, 2003) p. 259
369   Wikipedia: Yakuza. Online at http://en.wikipedia.org/wiki/Yakuza

treason against the nation, his kobuns must do the duty to look after the traitor. The *code of jingi* among Yakuza society demands the members to follow Oyabun's order regardless of the consequence he faces after obeying the order.

Woes & Pains Caused by Ultra-nationalism Today

At the end of this chapter we could ask the following questions: Did the most recent prime minister's visitation to Yasukuni create the danger of Japan's remilitarization in the same way as prior to the Second World War era? If no, then, what is the real danger? The real danger, in my personal view, is a psychosocial impact on the public, or waking up of a monster called "nationalism." The new monster would not intend the military aggression like the earlier one but it would keep the land purely "Japanese" and exclude foreign influences and foreigners from Japan as much as they could and make Japan a "real" independent nation-state like *NeverNeverLand*. There is a growing concern that the ultra-nationalist political view maintained by right wing politicians and business executives continues to get more and more approval from the public. Japan's new nationalism would not promote military expenditure; however, there is a danger that it could create narcissistic national or ethnic exclusivism.

Some say that Japan needs a healthier kind of nationalism. In my own personal view, however, all kind of nationalism is obsolete, futile and useless in this era of globalization, and even the concept of a nation-state seems outdated. We are moving in the direction of dissolving borders and the framework of nation-states, and towards the formation of a one world government. It has long been discussed in some Christian circles that the one world government is linked with the anti-Christ, therefore Christians should never agree with the idea to dissolve nation-states. However, such a view is completely without foundation as it is based on a wrong interpretation of the Scripture and has no academic rationale. The anti-Christ will come sooner or later but his arrival had nothing to do with a one world government that might bring us more convenience, and abetter life and prosperity based on global cooperation.

Many prominent and influential people in Japan's establishment like Takatoku Nakajo regarded that "the end of their country was the end of the world." The existence of the nation-state and the emperor system was *raison d'etre* or the ultimate meaning of life. Just like the holographic people in *StarTrek,* they were not able to live without a large computer system called the nation-state or Kokutai. This could well be due to the fact that they never met the true God who stands beyond the border of any nation-state and can provide true security in the spiritual realm. For believers of Christ, citizenship on earth is only a temporal arrangement and nothing compared to the ultimate citizenship in God's kingdom. People without this ultimate citizenship tend to seek for a false security and sense of belonging to earthly kingdoms.

The new nationalism could only produce economical woes, recessions, depressions and poverties even worse than Soviet Russia or any past or present totalitarian regime.

[370] Ohma from the comic version of Nausicaä: Is he a good God Warrior? Hayao Miyazaki.[371]

370   Was available June 2010; http://img02.hamazo.tv/usr/
      kanzin/%E6%A1%9C%E8%8A%B1.jpg
371   The picture is used under "fair dealing" (Canada) and "fair use" (USA)
      provisions in copyright law.

CHAPTER 10

GLOBALIZATION, POST-MODERNITY & DEATH OF NATION-STATES

All Empires are Illusions

[372]According to Richard Appignanesi and Chris Garratt (1995/2005), we live in the Post-modern era characterized by globalization, absence of borders between nation-states, and a nontraditional view of reality and ultimate consumerism. I am strongly convinced that in the era of globalization, any event happening in one portion of the globe will affect other parts, because many regions of the entire planet are now connected with each other in networks like neurons in a brain. Events happening in Japan are not events in a different home world like the Planet Kronos where Klingons came from, totally unrelated to the life we have in North America, but impact our life here either directly or indirectly. For instance, if there is an economic chaos or depression in Asia as the result of a conflict between China and Japan, what kind of impact would Canadian and U.S. economy have? Almost all industries with trading relationships with Asian nations would have either major or minor damages. All booming construction industries in Vancouver, B.C. could fall into a serious recession or even depression. Therefore, in the era we live in, we could safely assert that there is no independent nation-state in many different senses.

[373]Ryumei Yoshimoto[374] (吉本隆明) (1972) characterized the concept of nation-state as a "common fantasy" or illusion as well as the idea that the emperor symbolized the unity of the

372   Richard Appignanes, Garratt, Chris, et al. Introducing Postmodernism, (Canbridge, UK: Icon Books, 1995/2005) p. 187

373   Wikipedia吉本隆明. Online at http://ja.wikipedia.org/wiki/%E5%90%89%E6%9C%AC%E9%9A%86%E6%98%8E

374   Ryumei Yoshimoto. Kyodo genso ron [Study of a common fantasy]. Yoshimoto Ryumei zen chosaku Shu (Tokyo: Keiso Shobo, 1972)

Japanese nation, people and culture. Nation-states still existed in the early 21st century, however with much less power and significance than previous centuries. They lost their potency and significant role in the globe like Uranus as the result of emasculation by his son Cronos. The global capitalism and post-modern commercialism have castrated their predecessors, the nation-states, which formerly possessed the de facto force and control over the life of all human subjects, in the same way as Cronos slashed the penis of his father.

The term anachronism could well describe the status of nation-states and nationalism in the 21st century. After losing their potency, all individual states on the earth are treated as mere illusions or holograms created in cyber-space or a theme park like Disney World.

Thus, all nation-states in a traditional sense have already died out in a globalized community a little more than 100 years after [375]Karl Marx predicted the outcome of the 19th century capitalism. We have only regional communities that look like independent states under one global capitalism. Some of them still have a powerful appearance with a strong military like United States or China. But they are powerless in the face of global corporations or capitals, since militaries could not operate without the technologies created by the industries. In the 20th century, industries are under the leash of governments. But no governments of individual states are able to control the industries in the following century. The fascinating reality is that at the beginning of the 21st century, the CEO of Microsoft, Toyota, Sony or Apple Computer have more power and de facto force than the president of the United States or China, or prime minister of Japan or the UK.

Next, all realities were becoming relative and the sense of the ultimate reality would disappear in the post-modern world. [376]*Inception* (2010) is an American science fiction film created by Christopher Nolan (b. 1970). In this film people can sleep in close proximity connected by a sedative administering device and

375   Wikipedia: Karl Marx. Online at http://en.wikipedia.org/wiki/Karl_Marx
376   Wikipedia: Inception (film). Online at http://en.wikipedia.org/wiki/Inception_(film)

drug. The protagonist Dom Cobb played by Leonardo DiCaprio (b. 1974) is on an extraction mission within the mind of powerful businessman performs a form of corporate espionage through dreams. Cobb's mind is continually haunted by his deceased wife Mal by Marion Cotillard and she sabotages his missions. This is based on a post-modernist assumption that dream is another reality that is as real as a waking life. The reality in post-modernity is as relativistic as the one in the famous "butterfly dream" of [377]*Zhuangzi* (莊子). He wrote that:

> Once Chuang Chou dreamt he was a butterfly,
> a butterfly flitting and fluttering around, happy
> with himself and doing as he pleased. He
> didn't know he was Chuang Chou. Suddenly
> he woke up and there he was, solid and
> unmistakable Chuang Chou. But he didn't
> know if he was Chuang Chou who had dreamt
> he was a butterfly, or a butterfly dreaming he
> was Chuang Chou. Between Chuang Chou and
> a butterfly there must be *some* distinction!
> This is called the Transformation of Things.

Just like Zhuangzi the ancient Chinese philosopher and poet who lived around the 4th century BCE, the post-modern philosophers in the late 20th and early 21st centuries are open to the possibility that both dream and the waking life can be equally reality or non-reality since their philosophical assumption is based on extreme scepticism.

According to [378]James P. Danaher, post-modernists argue that the cornerstones of modernity, which includes a materialist and mechanical view of nature and an assumption that we can know reality objectively is both unrealistic and undesirable. He also contends that science has continued to produce evidence that makes the materialist, mechanical worldview ever more

377   Wikipedia: Zhuangzi. Online at http://en.wikipedia.org/wiki/Zhuang_Zi
378   James P. Danaher. Postmodern Christianity and the Reconstruction of the Christian Mind. (Bethesda, MD: Academic Press, 2001) pp. 5-6

unrealistic. The world is more complex than the model of modernity allows, and our understanding of it is never objective but always subjective and relativistic. It is a form of ultimate scepticism and *Copernican Revolution* that could totally demolish scientism, dialectic materialism, naturalistic evolutionalism and traditional Western rationalism. Scholars from the 18th century boldly postulated there was nothing supernatural, spiritual world or life after death even without any evidence to prove their assumptions.

Post-historical World

The post-modern world was also considered to be the post-historical world or the world after history. [379]Francis Fukuyama (1992/2006) named the era of globalization *post-history* or the history after modern history, in which nation-states had lost their potency. All powerful nations are about to sink under the horizon and the borderless global community and one-world-government emerge. According to Fukuyama, democratic and highly industrialized nations in the 1980s belonged to the post-historical world, while China, Soviet Russia and Islamic nations ruled by dictators still belonged to the old historical-world. They were nations still dominated by nationalism, political ideologies or religious dogmas, and large territories of the globe were still like that in the 1980s. However, the territory of the post-historical world continued to expand - China after the Tianammen Square protests of 1989 and Russia after the fall of Soviet Union in 1991, joined the post-historical world. In the mid 2000s, only a few nations including North Korea and Iran still belong to the historical-world according to Fukuyama's definition. Regarding the nation-state and nationalisms, he contends:

> The post-historical world would still be divided
> into nation-states, but its separate nationalisms
> would have made peace with liberalism and
> would express themselves increasingly in the
> sphere of private life alone. Economic rationality,

---

379   Francis Fukuyama. The End of History and the Last Man. (New York, USA: Free Press, 1992/2006) p. 276

in the meantime, will erode many traditional
features of sovereignty as it unifies markets
and production (Fukuyama, 1992/2006).

In other words, Fukuyama maintains that in the post-historical world, nation-state and nationalism are allowed to exist within a limitation and under strict control of global capitalism. If they crossed the line and harmed the welfare of the global community, they would be terminated immediately.

After Fukuyama first published his book in 1992, the territory of the "historical world" diminished significantly, and almost became annihilated. In the post-modern era, however, the old historical-world could continue to exist in a private and virtual reality instead of the physical space. In the post-historical world, all nationalism or patriarchism of any nationality will soon be relics. But relics might retain their values and be preserved in a museum in cyber-space.

Post-Modern View on the Reality & Japan's Emperor Cult

Dealing with counter-productive historical relics including Japan's ultra-nationalism, there is one potentially large problem in the era of Post-modernity and Post-history according to Fukuyama's definition. Japan's ultra-nationalism propagated by institutions like Yasukuni Shrine was highly anti-social and nearly impossible to co-exist with the post-historical world ruled by the democracy and capitalism. However, in the post-modern world, there is a possibility that Yasukuni's world-view or any other twisted view on the history could easily obtain approval and citizenship in the global community as one of many alternatives. That is, until it causes problems by violating the rule of the post-modernity and post-historical world, which allowed nationalism to express itself in the sphere of private life alone.

When we discuss the post-modern way of viewing human history, we must deal with three separate topics. One is dealing with the multiplicity of interpretations of the same reality and another one is the existence of multiple realities. Thirdly, we have to deal with artificial or created reality in post-modernity.

[380]According to Richard Appignanesi and Chris Garratt (1995/2005), the Post-modern era is characterized by the reproducibility of the reality and consumerism. In the post-modern world, artificially created reality like cyber-space or a theme park such as Disney World can be as real or unreal as the reality outside. The post-modernist view is that even our waking life or the reality we are in can not be as real as we assume, just as the dream of Chuang Chou, which *Zhuangzi* was referring to over 2,000 years ago.

As I have stated in the previous chapters, Japan's ultra-nationalists had exhibited a slanted view of Japan's military history, with highlights of heroic moments, justified aggressions on China and surrounding regions of East Asia, telling the public that Kamikaze pilots were true heroes who died for the divine emperor, the country of Kami and a great cause to liberate the East Asia from the Western domination.

Such a view could be one acceptable option to understand the same historical facts in the post-modern world. Also, since post-modernism does not view human history necessarily in a linear fashion and is open to the existence of multiplicity of realities and histories, post-modernists might postulate that Yasukuni Shrine's historians were quoting the facts in a different reality from some parallel universe. In the post-modern way of thinking characterized by the ultimate form of relativism and scepticism, one must be open to all different alternatives, since there is no standard of absolute right or wrong, and existence of only one historical reality.

In the reality we are in, it is an established fact that Japan's military invaded China and all her neighbors. Also, according to an interpretation of this historical fact in a standard history textbook, Japan's military aggression demolished all of China, her surroundings and a huge area of East Asia. Post-modern philosophical assumption is open to alternative interpretation of the facts. Post-modernism does not deny the possibility of an alternative historical philosophy that Japan was the key to the

---

380   Richard Appignanes, Garratt, Chris, et al. Introducing Postmodernism, (Canbridge, UK: Icon Books, 1995/2005) p. 48

liberation of other Asian countries from the U.S. and European powers, depending on a viewer's perspectives. They are also open to the possibility that there might be completely different historical realities in a different universe. Post-modernism boldly states the possibility Class-A War Criminals who committed heinous crimes were heroes in some other reality. It does not deny the possibility that a serial killer could be a hero in some other reality in some other universe.

The reason that no American leaders criticized Koizumi's Yasukuni visit or President George W. Bush even considered visiting there, lies in the fact that contemporary United States and Canada already belong to the era of post-modernity and the domain of post-history that holds the multiplicity of histories and realities. In post-modern USA, the history that American and Allied Forces fought for freedom and democracy was one of many realities, but not the only reality. Post-modernism does not assume that only one interpretation of history is correct. They are open to a revisionist worldview that states that Roosevelt was a warmonger who really wanted the war against the [381]Evil Axis. Some view that Admiral Yamamoto's plan to attack Pearl Habor was successful because Roosevelt made the security loose in the same way as Bush could have done for the attack on September 11, 2001. Japanese *uyoku* or ultra-nationalists portrayed Japan as the key to the liberation of other Asian countries from the U.S. and European powers.

Post-modernism accepted the multiplicity of realities and multiple interpretations of the same reality. Post-modern USA was pleased to accept alternative realities and histories including the one created by Yasukuni and Japanese ultra-nationalists, as long as they did not contradict with global capitalism. The multiplicity of histories and realities are like a huge shopping mall with stores to sell histories and realities. One historical interpretation is nothing more than a cinema DVD that consumers can purchase and experience a reality from it. Each person is expected to live in his or her own separate, personal history and reality and any two are not connected to

---

381   Wikipedia: Axis of evil. Online at http://en.wikipedia.org/wiki/Axis_of_evil

each other at all. It could also be like a Sony or Nintendo game in which one could be a Japanese Kamikaze pilot, while the same person could play the role of American freedom fighter when he or she was playing a different scenario. They accepted Yasukuni's alternative history in the same way they accepted homosexuality which is also called an alternative lifestyle.

[382]Appignanesi and Garratt postulate the Post-modern era can reproduce new realities in cyber-space or a completely fictional world. In the post-modern world, the alternative reality that Yasukuni created could be sustained as long as it was consumable as merchandise. Post-modernism scrapped the traditional Western values and standard of the ethics along with the traditional definition of reality. Post-modern USA did not care how Japan's ultra-nationalism or Islamic fundamentalism contradicted the traditional value system in the West because it was based on pure consumerism. Appignanesi and Garratt postulated Post-modernism meant "working without rules in order to find out the rules."

From the post-modern consumerism perspective, the revisionist view of Japan's military history could be utilized in the video game business, in which customers play the role of the heroic Japanese soldier. The game is created under the assumption that Kamikaze pilots were true heroes who died for the divine emperor, the country of Kami and a great cause to liberate the East Asia from the Western domination. However, both American and Chinese youth could play the role of heroic Kamikaze soldiers without contradicting their own consciences as it is simply a game. In the world of *Play Station*, people could have all kinds of roles and identity with the same assumption as [383]William Shakespeare (1564–1616) who stated, "[384]All the world's a stage and we are merely players." In the extension of this assumption, our personal, national or ethnic identities

382   Richard Appignanes, Garratt, Chris, et al. Introducing Postmodernism, (Canbridge, UK: Icon Books, 1995/2005) p. 48
383   Wikipedia: William Shakespeare. Online at http://en.wikipedia.org/wiki/Shakespere
384   William Shakespeare. As You Like It. (London, UK: Penguin Classics, 1599/1959)

are merely roles that we play in a stage or *Play Station*, and therefore we are ready to switch roles any time.

A video game is a quick disappearing reality like the dream of Chuang Chou, which *Zhuangzi* was referring to over 2,000 years ago, and destined to disappear when people finished the game. In a dream, one could be a serial killer, mass-murderer, or ruthless dictator, then this person could return to the waking life with no remorse for what he or she did in a dream reality. Likewise, no one would feel remorse for what he or she had done in the world of a video game, unless this person was neurotic or severely disturbed.

Alternative History Shinzo Abe's Parallel Universe

According to analysts, Prime Minister Abe promises to refrain from high-profile visits to Yasukuni Shrine as he privately discusses with Chinese leaders shortly after the installation to his office, although he could perhaps make personal visits without publicity. Japan's business groups have put heavy pressure on Abe to refrain himself from the Yasukuni, which has jeopardized growing business ties between Japan and China. It is one good thing that he had to comply with his patrons with better commonsense than he has, even if it's unwilling this time.

However, Abe had not given up his nationalist belief and agreement with the teachings Yasukuni Shrine propagated. Although he has refrained himself from an official visit to Yasukuni because he is aware of the detrimental effects on the diplomacy with China and South Korea, he continues to maintain the personal alliance with the shrine and ultranationalist supporters. It has been discovered that [385]Abe sent an offering to the Yasukuni Shrine in late April 2007 in his "private capacity" and the Japanese government therefore had no comment. Foreign Minister Taro Aso said separately he saw little possibility of Abe's action harming Japanese relations with China and South Korea, which have been angered by the visits of Japanese officials,

---

385   Kyodo News. LEAD: Shiozaki says Abe sent offering to Yasukuni in 'private capacity'. Yahoo Asian News. May. 2007. Online at http://asia.news.yahoo.com/070508/kyodo/d8ovvpd80.html

including former Prime Minister Junichiro Koizumi, to Yasukuni in the past. Hidenao Nakagawa (born 1945), secretary general of Abe's ruling *Liberal Democratic Party*, also defended Abe's action, calling it strictly "private." The Japanese government's top spokesman confirmed that no public funds were used in making the offering. Nakagawa also stated the prime minister explained his thoughts about Yasukuni Shrine visits to the leaders of China and South Korea and had gained their understanding, therefore there should be no significant diplomatic impact caused by his action.

But according to Yasukuni Shrine, Abe offered a potted "masakaki" plant worth 50,000 yen to the shrine on the occasion of its April 21-23 spring festival for Shinto rituals using his official title and a wooden plate attached to the pot read, "Prime Minister Shinzo Abe." Mizuho Fukushima (born 1955), leader of the opposition *Social Democratic Party*, slammed Abe for sending what she called "double-tongued" messages favoring China as well as domestic Yasukuni supporters.

[386]Abe also made a stunning statement to deny the existence of "[387]comfort women" or sex-partners for soldiers that Japanese military held during the Pacific War. The news said Abe was not only denying his own government's previous statements about "comfort women," but also ignoring the evidence researched by UN bodies and international human rights organizations such as *Amnesty International*. A former "comfort woman" from Australia testified that she and nine other young women were taken to a house in Java and used as a brothel by the Japanese military. For the next three months, they were raped repeatedly by soldiers. In March 2007, *Friends of Comfort Women in Australia* rallied at the Japanese consulate in Sydney.

[388]Abe stated he would not apologize for the sexual enslavement of captive women in the Second World War even

386   Stephen Moynihan. Abe ignores evidence, say Australia's 'comfort women'. The Age. March. 2007. Online at http://www.theage.com.au
387   Wikipedia: Comfort women. Online at http://en.wikipedia.org/wiki/Comfort_women
388   Peter Alford. Abe not sorry on comfort women. The Australian. March. 2007. Online at http://www.theaustralian.news.com.au

if the US Congress demanded it. He claimed that there was not evidence of coercion in the extreme sense of kidnapping that forced women to serve as sex-slaves. Abe insisted that if prostitution for soldiers ever existed during the war, these women served voluntarily in brothels organized by private contractors instead of any division of the Imperial military of government organizations. Abe changed his stance once and softened his position to accept the existence of prostitution in the military. He was adamant, however, not to admit the fact that these women were coerced to offer sexual intercourse to soldiers. Abe consistently insisted that these women chose to sell their bodies so that they could make a living. According to him, although their living conditions might have forced them to serve as comfort women, neither Japanese government nor military organizations coerced them to do so. He was ready to express an apology for Japanese military as indirectly responsible for the condition that these women had no choice to sell themselves, but not they were coerced to have sex with soldiers.

But according to the established record of history based on the research following traditional methodology, the existence of "comfort women" during the war is an objective reality and established fact and so Abe's denial is outrageous and unspeakable. Apart from Abe's explanation, these women were forced to serve as military comforters. His adamant denial gives an appearance that Abe resides in a different reality that would say Japan fought a righteous war to liberate the entire East Asia from the evil U.S. and European forces. Because Imperial Japan is the righteous force in his reality, any evil deed like forced prostitution is impossible to exist.

Former "comfort women" from Australia and various parts of Asia had vivid memory of rapes, abuses and forced prostitutions. However, Abe did not find any reasons for an apology to them because he came from a completely different historical reality. In the reality that he lives, there is no such thing as forced prostitutions by the Japanese military. In the alternative reality from some other universe Abe grew up these women never existed.

Dealing with the issues of Yasukuni Shrine and the "comfort women", Abe seems to have followed a typical post-modernist way of thinking that accepts a multiplicity of historical realities and multiple interpretations of one reality. Dealing with Yasukuni, he was most likely adopting the revisionist interpretation or simply interpreting differently the same historical reality that we know. The only explanation of his action or where he is coming from is that he lived in a different reality, unless he is insane or mentally disabled. In a traditional modernist logic, to value science and hold on to only one historical reality, there is no way to justify what Japanese military did to these women, since there is no way to erase and rewrite the record that was already established as facts.

Kizo Ogura (2006)[389] maintains both Koizumi and Abe belonged to a group of people called *orechin* (おれちん) characterized by their typically post-modern lifestyle and way of thinking. They are extremely individualistic, but not in the same way as Westerners whose basic habitat is external reality outside of fantasy. The *orechin* or Japanese post-modernists according to Ogura are extraordinarily private and live in their own reality and do not care about the reality outside. Since Koizumi was *orechin* with no interest in external reality, he did not care how much his visits to Yasukuni enraged Chinese and Koreans and damaged Japan's economy as well as her relationship with neighbors. In the same way, Abe denied the existence of the comfort women for Japanese soldiers since he was also *orechin* who only cared about his personal reality. Both Koizumi and Abe lived in the historical realities that Yasukuni propagated in which Japan fought a righteous war and played a vital role to liberate the Asia from Western oppression.

Ogura also maintains that while Koizumi is an older type of *orechin*, Abe was the [390]*Newtype,* or mutated, and more evolved version of *orechin*. He is a post-modernist propagating a pre-modern nationalist ideology with a much stronger tone

---

389   Ogura, Kizo. Orechin [Me in the personal reality] (Tokyo: Asahi Shimbun, 2006)
390   Wikipedia: Newtype. Online at http://en.wikipedia.org/wiki/Newtype

than Koizumi. He wrote a book [391]*Utsukushii Kuni e* (美し
い国へ) "Toward a Beautiful Country" (2006) expressing a
hawkish stance on revising Japan's pacifist constitution and the
legitimacy of the Japanese prime minister's visits to Yasukuni.
Ogura contends that Abe's political stance had regressed to
the pre-modern era from the post-modernity. But his thinking
patterns are solidly post-modern although his political ideology
is pre-modern nationalism. He is a person who lives in his own
virtual reality instead of the external world and perceives himself
as prime minister of Japan in a different universe from the one
in which we live.

Therefore, we could safely assume that Abe was the first
Japanese Prime Minister with acompletely different mindset
from any one among his predecessors. He must have totally
abandoned the modernist way of thinking or views on history
and acted upon the post-modern political philosophy with the
acceptance of multiplicity of realities and the bold assumption
that there was no absolute one and only historical reality. In
post-modernism there is no absolute reality and all realities are
relativistic and ultimate illusions, so Abe is free to create any
reality he wishes.

[392]Appignanesi and Garratt state that Disneyland
represented the post-modern reality. The reality, according to
post-modern definition, is nothing more than an electronically
created theme park. In this sense, Abe has a legitimate right
to create his own reality in a virtual space in which the Imperial
Japanese Army and Navy fought a righteous war against evil
Western Imperialism. If he were the prime minister of Japan in
some parallel universe with a different historical reality in which
his claim was an established fact, he could safely profess his
personal view on the history in his official capacity.

According to the post-modern way of viewing reality, both
our universe and the one that Abe came from are legitimate and

---

391 Shinzo Abe. Utsukushii Kuni e [Toward a Beautiful Country] (Tokyo:
      Bungeishunju, 2006)
392 Richard Appignanes, Garratt, Chris, et al. Introducing Postmodernism,
      (Canbridge, UK: Icon Books, 1995/2005) p. 121

acceptable as real worlds. If Abe resided in a universe in which comfort women of the Imperial Japanese military never existed in history, the post-modern political philosophy would tell him, "So, be it." The US authority could not judge him for expressing a value system, which contradicted their own traditional values, because it did not contradict with the post-modern and post-historical consumerism.

The real danger of Abe's leadership, however, is that he might attempt persuade as many Japanese citizens as possible to migrate into his reality through the [393]wormhole he created. Ogura maintains that Abe's book was quite persuasive among younger post-modern generation in Japan and an effective tool to induce them to the "beautiful country" of his own reality. He gained popularity as he spoke against the government of North Korea when the media discovered that Japanese citizens had been kidnapped to North Korea by its secret agents. But one could say Abe was guilty of kidnapping people into the universe he came from through from his wormhole, telling them the state of Japan in his own reality was a "beautiful country" or utopia that no one had ever seen, using the same tactics and propaganda as North Korean government employed.

If Abe started professing that what he had believed was the one and only reality, it might mean he was returning to the modernist or traditional way of viewing the reality. It would obviously contradict with the post-modern relativism, so that the post-modern global capitalism would not tolerate him anymore. In the post-modern and post-historical world, multiplicity of realities are accepted, and no one could claim that his or her own reality was the one and only acceptable reality because it was against the golden rule of relativism and pluralism. If Abe abandons the post-modernist stance in viewing the reality, but retains the ultra-nationalist stance in viewing the history, he would instantaneously lose support not only from China and South Korea but also the United States, Japan's long lasting strongest ally and supporter after the Second World War.

393   Wikipedia: Wormhole. Online at http://en.wikipedia.org/wiki/Wormhole

The historical reality that General Toshio Tamogami presented in his controversial article described in Chapter 8 is also an acceptable reality according to the post-modernist perspective that is open to the existence of a multiplicity of realities and histories. He may be considered one of those who travelled from a different historical reality in a different universe. In the reality that Tamogami came from, his country was not an "aggressor nation" during the Second World War but rather considered it an established fact that Japan was tricked into involvement by the United States and President Roosevelt. Also, pre-war Japan was a fully democratic state with freedom of speech in which every citizen, including a uniformed general, could express opinions contradicting his or her government. Therefore, Japan's involvement in the war was for the sake of justice and freedom of Asian nations from the Western oppressors, and what Yasukuni's *Yushukan War Memorabilia Museum* presents is the historical fact as seen by Japan.

Emperor Cult & Kokutai Ideology in Post-modernity

According to the established fact of the reality we are in, Prime Minister Kiichiro Hiranuma's government passed and enacted an oppressive, blasphemous and abominable *Religious Organizational Law* in 1940. In the post-modern way of interpretation, there must be several different ways of seeing it. However, from the perspective of Christian values, the enactment of the Religious Organizational Law was nothing more than "pure evil." For Christians, a Religio-Political system that held the emperor as an inviolable sacred divinity was totally blasphemous and intolerable. It was grievous fact that many Christians were imprisoned for not complying with the blasphemous *Kokutai* system before the Second World War, particularly under Kiichiro Hiranuma's government. *Kokutai* was an evil nation-wide system in which all citizens of Japan were imposed to accept State Shinto and an emperor centred ideology. It demanded citizens profess belief in the myth that the emperor was descended from the Sun Goddess, in the same way as Rome demanded her citizens believe in Caesar's divinity. Otherwise, they were either imprisoned as traitors and criminals against the peace and national unity or conscripted to the army as the lowest ranking soldiers and deleted in the battlefield. In summary, the sociological DNA of State Shinto, Kokutai and Japan's emperor system was programmed to "[394]kill, steal and destroy" and there were nothing good in it.

Also, from the perspective of ordinary citizens, it was extremely difficult to view Kiichiro Hiranuma as anyone except purely evil, possibly demonized. But Yasukuni Shrine's Yushukan Museum viewed him as one of the heroes who gave their lives to the greater cause. In light of post-modern philosophy, it could be a different way of interpreting the same reality that Hiranuma created. Alternatively, it could mean a heroic act of a "good Hiranuma" from a different universe, or completely fictional Hiranuma that Yushukan created in their cyber-space. The first interpretation was most problematic since it condoned all evil acts he did in this reality and praised them as heroic. The second of the interpretations could be harmless as long as it differentiated a good Hiranuma of the alternative or fictional reality from the evil one in our reality.

Japan's State Shinto was a nation-wide cult to which all citizens had to submit. The formation of the *Kamikaze Party* indicated that Japan's State Shinto was a dangerous cult organization. The military leaders of the Imperial Japan pressured young men with a long future head of them to pilot pieces of technology built for suicide missions and to crash them into American aircraft carriers to perform a type of Shinto *Jihad*. They could have used rhetoric like: *Real man must go Kamikaze*, or *It's an ultimate way to please your parents because you are becoming a god*. The Imperial government imposed the whole Japanese nation to blind submission to the leadership and were asked to sacrifice their lives for the great victory or the larger good, saying that they were greatly rewarded as *Kami* or deified super-being in afterlife. They had a similar social and psychological structure as the entire organization of al-Qaeda that attacked the World Trade Centre in 2001 and employed the same method as *Kamikaze Party*.

---

394   John 10:10

After the Second World War, the oppressive *Kokutai* and State Shinto were dismantled. Citizens of Japan and her neighbours enjoyed peace and freedom without any ideology imposed upon them. However, the DNA of the *Kokutai* system and Emperor Cult were not completely destroyed, though dormant after the war. Because the emperor system and ultra-nationalist groups were still there, we cannot completely deny chances of their resurrection. By pushing prime ministers to visit and worship Kami in Yasukuni, Japan's ultra-nationalists and followers of Yasukuni cult were constantly trying to resurrect pre-war Siamese Twin Monster, Japan's State Shinto and *Kokutai* from the bottom of Hades like God Warriors in Nausicaä of the Valley of the Wind," by Hayao Miyazaki.

CHAPTER 11

THE END OF BABYLONS
CONCLUSION

The ultra-nationalist movement and Shinto Cult around Yasukuni Shrine in Japan are facing a new phase as the modernist assumptions from the 19th century bankrupted. After the Second World War, Japan's ultra-nationalists held a slanted, revisionist and non-standard view of Japan's military history with highlights of heroic moments, justified aggressions on China and surrounding regions, romanticized Kamikaze suicide missions and the denial of almost all wartime atrocities that Japanese soldiers committed. They were telling the Japanese public and the global community that Kamikaze pilots were true heroes who died for the divine emperor, the country of Kami and a great cause to liberate East Asia from the evil Western domination. In the era of post-modernity such interpretation could be accepted either as a different interpretation of the same historical facts in the same reality, or a completely different reality from a different universe.

Also, all nation-states in a traditional sense are going to die out in a globalized post-modern world a little more than 100 years after Karl Marx predicted the outcome of the 19th century capitalism. We are going to have only regional communities that look like independent nation-states under one global capitalism and all nationalism will be treated as mere relics. But nation-states and nationalisms will continue to exist in a personalized virtual reality after being expelled from the three-dimensional world, since relics must have commercial values as museum displays and video game programs in which people can relive the past events their forefathers experienced. In post-modernity, both virtual realities and three dimensional external realities are equally real and unreal.

Post-modernism postulated the existence of multiple realities from multiple universes and these realities and universes had no mutual communication.

As long as Japanese *uyoku* or followers of the nationalist Emperor Cult stay in their new virtual space, they will peacefully coexist with the post-modern world ruled by the global capitalism.

End of Piscean Age, War Gods & Empires

During the Second World War, it appears that in the conflict between Japan and the U.S., there was no righteous side. Both seemed to have been fighting out of greed and ego satisfaction. The United States was more concerned with the imperialistic expansion of its own territory rather than world peace, democracy and freedom of other nation states. It is a historical fact that the United States continued to expand their colonies in the 19th and 20th centuries, in some ways similar to the Old World suzerain regimes of Europe. The U.S. colonized Hawaii and Philippines and other small nations around the Pacific Rim as a type of continued imperialistic venture. They also condoned their own nationalism, racial discrimination and segregation. It is a well known fact that US residents with Japanese origin were sent to concentration camps for no other reason than they were of Japanese origin.

Even after the war, African Americans were not given full US citizenship until the 1960s shortly before Martin Luther King and John F. Kennedy were assassinated. This could parallel Judges 21:25 that describes the days that Israel had no king; everyone did as he saw fit.

Such a dark side of U.S. history fostered the negative energy of Japanese militarists to wage war against the United States and her allies. It gave Tojo and other leaders of the Imperial Japan a justification to start the "war on racism" as stated in the web site and pamphlets from the Yasukuni Shrine.

In my conclusion, both Axis and Allied sides were "Babylons" or evil empires during this war. Nevertheless, the defeat of Imperial Japan along with Nazi Germany and the resultant termination of the evil regime was a significant historical event in human history ordained by our God. In his sermon John Neufeld (2010), the senior pastor of Willingdon Church, Burnaby BC. maintains that God is sovereign over evils, and uses them for his own purposes, although he is not responsible for their existence. God raised and used Babylonia and Assyria, a couple of evil empires in the ancient Near East to punish his own people in Israel who went wayward and became as evil as pagans. However, he destroyed both empires at the end. It was his intention to destroy the Imperial Japan and Hirohito's regime before destroying the racism of the United States. Isaiah 10 states that God will use evil nations for the purpose of his fury and destroy them after that.

Habakkuk repeated the phrase "Woe to Babylon" in the second chapter of this book. "Babylon" the mighty capital of Babylonia is used as a symbolic term for powerful empires in ancient and modern days.

In the book of Daniel, King Nebuchadnezzar of Babylon had a dream of an extremely strange looking statue. [395]The head was made of pure gold, its chest and arms of silver, its belly and thighs of bronze, its legs of iron, and its feet partly of iron and partly of baked clay. Daniel the prophet interpreted that the part made of gold was the glorious and magnificent kingdom of Nebuchadnezzar. After that many powerful empires like the kingdom of silver, bronze, iron and clay followed. However, a huge rock came out from nowhere to smash and destroy all of them at the end. This story would vividly illustrate the destiny of all-powerful nations, empires or kingdoms and demonic totalitarian regimes on earth. Japan's pre-Second World War evil totalitarian government led by the cultic community of the Divine Emperor collapsed and passed away in the same way as one of empires in Nebuchadnezzar's dream. By the end of the 20th century, all nation-states lost their power and potency in front of global capitalism, just like Uranus was brutally castrated and dethroned by his son Cronos.

---

395   Daniel 2:32-33

My first book, *All The World Is Anime* (2010), includes a discussion regarding moving from the Era of Pisces, or the constellation of twin fish, into the Era of Aquarius or a constellation of a massive urn filled with water. Piscean Age is characterized by masculinity, i.e. the penis, perpetual aggression and conflicts, modernism, nationalism, imperialism and racially divided societies. On the other hand, Aquarian Age is characterized by femininity, i.e. the vagina, inclusiveness vs. exclusiveness, post-modernism, globalism and a post-racial world.

In fact, the Pisces icon, according to the Enlightenment philosophy and theology, could be seen as a large sea monster like Herman Melville's [396]*Moby-Dick*[397] (1851) or a gigantic phallic image that replaced Christ. Moby-Dick was a mottled sperm whale with a white hump, of extraordinary ferocity and size, but also possessed ineffable strength, mystery, and power. The novel describes the voyage of the whaling ship *Pequod*, commanded by Captain Ahab, who led his crew on a hunt for the great whale Moby-Dick. The book's language is highly symbolic, and many themes run throughout the work although the symbolism of the whale is not clear. Debate has gone on for over a century as to whether it is symbolic of nature, providence, fate, or even God.

We could have a few other plausible interpretations of the gigantic whale. As [398]Eyal Peretz (2003) states, Moby-Dick can indicate any extremely powerful object so the whale could also symbolize an extremely powerful ultimate phallus, to symbolize modernism or the Enlightenment philosophy that made men feel so potent and proud that they started thinking of themselves as God, since "Dick" could also refer to a penis. The whale could be another symbol of a monstrous modernism like Miyazaki's God Warrior that carries a mass destruction force. Modernist Christianity that followed the Enlightenment, unknowingly and

---

396   Herman Melville. Moby Dick: His Masquerade (Chicago, IL: NTC/Contemporary Publishing Company, 1851/1999)

397   Wikipedia: Moby-Dick. Online at http://en.wikipedia.org/wiki/Moby_Dick

398   Eyal Peretz. Literature, Disaster, and the Enigma of Power A Reading of 'Moby-Dick' (Stanford, CA: Stanford University Press, 2003)

unconsciously, worshipped the phallic symbol instead of the true savior. [399]John Lardas (2006) asserts that:

> According to Melville, the directives of "imperial selfhood," even though they had undergirded numerous projects of American modernity —from industry and the economy, religion and philosophy, to national infrastructures and mental scaffoldings — had already begun to fail (Lardas, 2006).

Lardas argues that in *Moby-Dick*, Melville explores, through the eyes of Captain Ahab, how the relentless pursuit of spiritual autonomy, epistemological clarity, and ocular dominion can eventually result in submission, confusion, and blindness. Cursing his "inter-indebtedness" to technology, Ahab became infused with its logic, admitting, "The path to my fixed purpose is laid with iron rails, where on my soul is grooved to run." Therefore, according to Lardas' perspective, Melville views Moby-Dick as a symbol of modernism and the quickly advancing technology that the modern era created.

My conclusion is that in the modern age, or the era of Enlightenment, all world leaders were acting like Captain Ahab of the whaling ship *Pequod*, chasing after *Moby-Dick, the great sperm whale which was the symbol of ineffable strength, mystery, and ultimate masculinity or phallic power.* However, the Pisces icon or the symbol of modernism, will be utterly demolished in the Aquarian Age.

The reality was that, as Prophet Jeremiah stated, [400]worshippers of feces gods were also destined to become a heap of waste or not be mourned or buried and be like "excrement" lying on the ground. For instance, Class-A war criminals who were accused and convicted in the Tokyo court by the *International Military Tribunal* in 1945 like Hideki Tojo, Kuniaki Koiso, Kiichiro Hiranuma and Toshio Shiratori and all others died like dogs and became feces. They were mourned by the followers of evil

---

399   John, Lardas. Deus in Machina Movet: Religion in the Age of Technological
      Reproductivity Journal Method & Theory in the Study of Religion, 2006
400   Jeremiah 16:4; 25:33

religions and enshrined as Kami in Yasukuni Shrine. However, in God's eyes, Yasukuni's deities were mere heaps of waste with no life. These Yasukuni deities along with symbols of modernism and imperialism from the West which represent the Piscean era will collapse and become a heap of feces on the ground.

Armour of God

As supernatural weapons are available to us to defeat evil spiritual forces, God had endowed us with the power and splendour of the [401]armour of God. The armour includes a girdle of truth, a breastplate of righteousness, a shield of faith, and a helmet of salvation and the sword. The "sword" is the word of God covered by the precious blood of Jesus and the most powerful weapon to defeat evil. The Epistle to the Hebrews states:

> [402]For the word of God is living and active.
> Sharper than any double-edged sword, it
> penetrates even to dividing soul and spirit,
> joints and marrow; it judges the thoughts
> and attitudes of the heart (Hebrew 4:12).

With the double-edged sword from the one and only God, one would be able to annihilate or utterly destroy Yasukuni's Kami, Imperial spirits of the emperor's household coming from Hades or the Land of Yomi, [403]forces of evil and the principalities of darkness and any other evil spiritual entities made of filth, and make them into a pile of excrement lying on the ground.

[404]Prophet Daniel declared, "In the time of those kings, the God of heaven will set up a kingdom that will never be destroyed, nor will it be left to another people. It will crush all those evil kingdoms and bring them to an end, but it will itself endure forever."

My conclusion is that the Yasukuni Shrine, a source of many controversies in the Far East for decades following the Second

401   Ephesians 6:10-24
402   Hebrews 4:12
403   Ephesians 6:12
404   Daniel 2:44

World War, will cease to exist in divine timing. It is a modern day example of "gates of Hades" through which massive destructive spiritual forces were coming from the darkest dimension of this universe and into which millions of human souls were swallowed. The dark energy came through it before and during the war, and continues to this day. However, as Jesus declared during his visit to Caesarea Philippi with his disciples, the gates of Hades will not prevail forever, and that includes Yasukuni. There will be a time in the future when God will take down these evil gates for good and close all accesses to [405]hell dimensions (Matthew 16:18).

[406]Yasukuni Shrine's Torii (main gate): Gates of Hades shall not prevail (Matthew 16:18).[407]

405   Buffyverse Wiki: Hell Dimension. Online at http://buffy.wikia.com/wiki/Hell_dimension
406   Was available July 2010; http://hdri.iwalk.jp/images/hdr_temple112.jpg
407   The picture is used under "fair dealing" (Canada) and "fair use" (USA) provisions in copyright law.

About the Author

Isao Ebihara, D.Phil. (Oxford Graduate School, TN), a native of Japan, has resided in Canada for over 20 years. He has been teaching Japanese language courses at Trinity Western University in British Colombia since the fall of 2002. His academic training encompasses theology, psychology and literature, and his interests include Japanese language, Asian animation and pop culture, culture and spirituality and religions and politics.

Dr. Ebihara has a thorough knowledge of Japanese anime culture and recognizes its great impact on the global community. In his 2010 book, *All the World is Anime: Religions, Myths & Spiritual Metaphors in the World of Japanimation & Manga*, he explored the philosophical and religious/spiritual background of the anime authors and stories and a history of their productions.

In this book, Dr. Ebihara makes a comparison of the cultural and historical components of Shinto religion to pop cultures including *anime* or Japanese animations and *manga* or Japanese comics, drawing upon the work of Alan J.P. Taylor's *populist* or *"anti-great man"* approach and Carl Jung's *archetype* theory.

SHINTO WAR GODS OF YASUKUNI SHRINE
THE GATES OF HADES AND JAPAN'S EMPEROR CULT

ISBN 978-1-935434-56-6

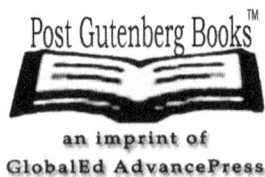

Post Gutenberg Books™

an imprint of
GlobalEd AdvancePress

www.ingramcontent.com/pod-product-compliance
Lightning Source LLC
Chambersburg PA
CBHW031257090426
42742CB00007B/489